NOAH
and the flood

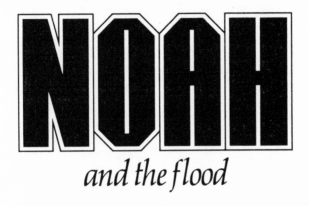

and the flood

Mark E. Petersen

Deseret Book Company
Salt Lake City, Utah

Library of Congress Cataloging in Publication Data

Petersen, Mark E.
  Noah and the flood.

  Includes index.
  1. Noah (Biblical figure) 2. Bible. O.T.—Biography.
3. Deluge. 4. Gabriel (Archangel). 5. Mormon Church—
Doctrinal and controversial works.
I. Title.
BX8643.N6P47 1982   222'.110924   [B]   82-14947
ISBN 0-87747-935-6

CONTENTS

Chapter One

AMONG THE GREATS

Noah, who built the ark, was one of God's greatest servants, chosen before he was born as were others of the prophets. He was no eccentric, as many have supposed. Neither was he a mythical figure created only in legend. Noah was real. The flood was real. And so was the ark, as were the various species of life saved in the ark. It was all factual, fully documented in scripture, and was the doing of the Almighty.

Let no one downgrade the life and mission of this great prophet. Noah was so near perfect in his day that he literally walked and talked with God.

This telestial planet of ours was destined to pass through three great crises. Two were related to the Savior: one to his second coming, the other to the time when the earth will be celestialized. But the third—which was first in order of events—was the flood in which Noah was the central figure. His choice for this strategic position is itself a measure of the greatness of this man and of the confidence placed in him by the Almighty.

Noah cried repentance to a wicked world, warning all men that they must change their ways or die in a deluge. They paid no heed. The prophecy was fulfilled, the ark was built, the flood came, and the earth was cleansed of its filth. After the waters receded, the world was made ready for a new generation of human beings to be propagated through Noah and his sons.

Few men in any age were as great as Noah. In many respects he was like Adam, the first man. Both had served as ministering angels in the presence of God even after

their mortal experience. Adam was Michael, the archangel, but Noah was Gabriel, one of those nearest to God.
Of all the hosts of heaven, he was chosen to open the
Christian era by announcing to Mary that she would become the mother of the Savior, Jesus Christ. He even
designated the name by which the Redeemer should be
known here on earth, saying He would be the Son of God.

The Prophet Joseph Smith properly identified Adam as
Michael and Noah as Gabriel. It was revealed to him that
Adam stands next to the Savior in the priesthood line, and
that Noah stands next to Adam, placing him in third
position from the Lord. (*History of the Church* 3:386.)

What a mighty figure Noah—Gabriel—must have
been in his premortal life! What a prophet in mortality!

We all had a premortal life, living as spirits in the
presence of God, our Eternal Father. As the Apostle Paul
taught on Mars Hill, we are the offspring of God, His
spirit children, and as Jesus taught, God is our Father.
Being His children, we lived with Him before the earth
was made. This planet was created to provide a home for
us while we are in this mortal life, which we call our
second estate. If we are successful here, the Lord has
promised that we shall return to His presence and literally
become like Him in eternity. Such is our potential destiny.

Michael, the chief of the angels, was chosen to begin
the human race. Only a tried and trusted personage would
be given such a responsibility. The task of sending all
mankind to a life on earth required a correct beginning.
Nothing less would do. The selection of our ultimate
progenitor, therefore, was all important. So Michael was
assigned. As the archangel, he crushed the rebellion of
Lucifer, and while leading the armies of heaven, he drove
Satan and his followers from the presence of our Heavenly Father.

Our Prophets have also told us that Michael assisted in
the creation of this earth. It was therefore most fitting that

he should be selected to serve as the first man and that we should become his posterity.

A task not unlike that assigned to Adam was given to Gabriel, who became Noah in mortality. Through His foreknowledge, the Lord knew the path that many of His children would follow on earth. He knew, too, which of the great premortal spirits would serve as his prophets to stabilize matters, teach His truth, and warn the wayward.

At critical periods in world history the Lord has always sent chosen servants with specific missions. These have included such men as Abraham, Isaac, Jacob, Joseph of Egypt, Moses, Joshua, Samuel, David, Jeremiah, Isaiah, Lehi, Nephi, Alma, and others of His great ones. Joseph Smith was chosen in this same manner to become God's prophet for the restoration of the gospel. There is nothing haphazard about our coming to earth. A spirit of great stature was required to begin the race, and the Lord provided him in the person of Michael, who became Adam.

In his foreknowledge, God knew that a second such individual would also be required, for he foresaw that most of Adam's children would reject the gospel and rebel as Satan would tell them, "Believe it not." Thus they would become carnal and sensual in those early years of the earth's history. The Lord knew that their wickedness would pollute the earth, and yet this same earth was intended as a home for the rest of God's children. Must they be born into a world of corruption?

The Savior had been appointed as our Redeemer in the primeval council in heaven. (See Moses 4:1-4; Abraham 3:27-28.) He, too, must be born here to accomplish His great atonement.

So the earth could not be utterly destroyed in being rid of its wicked inhabitants. It had only to be cleansed so that a righteous group could begin life here anew. The Lord decreed that his cleansing would be by water, a worldwide deluge. Therefore, from among his premortal spirit children, God chose another great individual—His third in line, Gabriel—to resume the propagation of mankind following the flood.

Such a one as Gabriel was needed because in mortality he would be more than a progenitor. He would be a champion of righteousness, a mighty prophet, a bulwark against the wickedness that would precede the flood. And he would be the prototype for the rest of humanity still awaiting birth after the cleansing of the earth by water.

Thus Gabriel was chosen to become Noah, a preacher of righteousness, the builder of the ark, the progenitor of the new beginning of mankind.

Chapter Two

GABRIEL'S MINISTRY

The angel Gabriel is spoken of in both Old and New Testaments of the Bible. To ancient prophets he was a firm reality, for he visited them. Certainly he was an important figure in the greatest event that ever happened, the mission of Christ.

It was he who opened the Christian era by heralding the forthcoming birth of the Savior of the world! In addition, he announced the rise of John the Baptist, who would prepare the way of the Lord. Centuries earlier he had visited the prophet Daniel and, as part of that miraculous event, had spoken of the Messiah, who was the Savior, Jesus Christ, the Son of God. (Daniel 8:16-27; 9:16-27.) He declared that Jerusalem would yet be built up to the name of the Messiah. He also assisted in the interpretation of the vision of Belshazzar.

Jews, Christians, and Arabs alike believe in the visitations of Gabriel. All Bible translations describe them and endorse them. However, only the Latter-day Saints, of all the peoples in the world, know that Gabriel became Noah of the flood.

Obviously, Gabriel's appearances to Daniel in Old Testament times and to Mary the mother of Jesus came long after the flood. He was not a resurrected person then, of course, because the resurrection came only after Christ himself had risen from the grave, for Jesus it was who broke the bands of death.

Gabriel's announcement of the forthcoming birth of the Lord occurred in this way:

"And in the sixth month the angel Gabriel was sent

from God unto a city of Galilee, named Nazareth, to a virgin espoused to a man whose name was Joseph, of the house of David; and the virgin's name was Mary.

"And the angel came in unto her, and said, Hail, thou that art highly favoured, the Lord is with thee: blessed art thou among women.

"And when she saw him, she was troubled at his saying, and cast in her mind what manner of salutation this should be.

"And the angel said unto her, Fear not, Mary: for thou hast found favour with God. And, behold, thou shalt conceive in thy womb, and bring forth a son, and shalt call his name JESUS. He shall be great, and shall be called the Son of the Highest: and the Lord God shall give unto him the throne of his father David: and he shall reign over the house of Jacob for ever; and of his kingdom there shall be no end.

"Then said Mary unto the angel, How shall this be, seeing I know not a man?

"And the angel answered and said unto her, The Holy Ghost shall come upon thee, and the power of the Highest shall overshadow thee: therefore also that holy thing which shall be born of thee shall be called the Son of God.

"And, behold, thy cousin Elisabeth, she hath also conceived a son in her old age: and this is the sixth month with her, who was called barren. For with God nothing shall be impossible." (Luke 1:26-37.)

Apparently the same angel appeared to Joseph, Mary's espoused husband, for Matthew says:

"Now the birth of Jesus Christ was on this wise: When as his mother Mary was espoused to Joseph, before they came together, she was found with child of the Holy Ghost. Then Joseph her husband, being a just man, and not willing to make her a publick example, was minded to put her away privily.

"But while he thought on these things, behold, the

angel of the Lord appeared unto him in a dream, saying, Joseph, thou son of David, fear not to take unto thee Mary thy wife: for that which is conceived in her is of the Holy Ghost. And she shall bring forth a son, and thou shalt call his name JESUS: for he shall save his people from their sins.'' (Matthew 1:18-21.)

An angel—possibly Gabriel still—appeared to Joseph, Mary's husband, after the birth of the child Jesus, and counseled him to take his family to Egypt to escape the wrath of King Herod. The passage reads: ''And when they were departed, behold, the angel of the Lord appeareth to Joseph in a dream, saying, Arise, and take the young child and his mother, and flee into Egypt, and be thou there until I bring thee word: for Herod will seek the young child to destroy him.'' (Matthew 2:13.)

The angel appeared again, as we read:

''But when Herod was dead, behold, an angel of the Lord appeareth in a dream to Joseph in Egypt, saying, Arise, and take the young child and his mother, and go into the land of Israel: for they are dead which sought the young child's life. And he arose, and took the young child and his mother, and came into the land of Israel.'' (Matthew 2:19-21.)

It is interesting that in these visitations the angel spoke to Joseph as the head of this little family, though Joseph was only the foster father of the child.

With respect to John the Baptist, we have this record of the appearance of Gabriel:

''And there appeared unto him an angel of the Lord standing on the right side of the altar of incense. And when Zacharias saw him, he was troubled, and fear fell upon him.

''But the angel said unto him, Fear not, Zacharias: for thy prayer is heard; and thy wife Elisabeth shall bear thee a son, and thou shalt call his name John. And thou shalt have joy and gladness; and many shall rejoice at his birth.

For he shall be great in the sight of the Lord, and shall drink neither wine nor strong drink; and he shall be filled with the Holy Ghost, even from his mother's womb. And many of the children of Israel shall he turn to the Lord their God. And he shall go before him in the spirit and power of Elias, to turn the hearts of the fathers to the children, and the disobedient to the wisdom of the just; to make ready a people prepared for the Lord.

"And Zacharias said unto the angel, Whereby shall I know this? for I am an old man, and my wife well stricken in years.

"And the angel answering said unto him, I am Gabriel, that stand in the presence of God: and am sent to speak unto thee, and to shew thee these glad tidings. And, behold, thou shalt be dumb, and not able to speak, until the day that these things shall be performed, because thou believest not my words, which shall be fulfilled in their season." (Luke 1:11-20.)

So Gabriel came as a ministering angel. He had served his mortal life as Noah, even as Michael had served his mortal life as Adam. Noah obviously had resumed his position as Gabriel just as Adam had resumed his position as Michael the Archangel in the eternal worlds.

Both of these personages came to the Prophet Joseph Smith as ministers of God. In section 128 of the Doctrine and Covenants, we read of the coming of both:

"And again, the voice of God in the chamber of old Father Whitmer, in Fayette, Seneca county, and at sundry times, and in divers places through all the travels and tribulations of this Church of Jesus Christ of Latter-day Saints! And the voice of Michael, the archangel; the voice of Gabriel, and of Raphael, and of divers angels, from Michael or Adam down to the present time, all declaring their dispensation, their rights, their keys, their honors, their majesty and glory, and the power of their priesthood; giving line upon line, precept upon precept; here a little, and there a little; giving us consolation by holding forth that which is to come, confirming our hope!" (D&C 128:21.)

It is interesting to note the expression "All declaring their dispensations, their rights, their keys, their honors, their majesty and glory and the power of their priesthood."

Peter the apostle had predicted that before the second coming of the Savior, there would be a restoration of all things that God had spoken by the mouths of all his holy prophets from the beginning of the world. (Acts 3:21.)

The visitations referred to in the Doctrine and Covenants indicate how it was done. There were other visitations also, including those of Moroni; John the Baptist; Peter, James, and John; Elijah; Moses; and Elias.

But the point we make here particularly is that both Michael (Adam) and Gabriel (Noah) came to the Prophet Joseph Smith and conferred keys upon him as other such visitors did. The Prophet indicated that Michael restored the keys of the First Presidency that he himself (Michael) held, and that he had obtained in the creation. (*History of the Church* 3:385-86.)

The keys restored by Noah would relate to the dispensation that he headed, but the detail has not been revealed.

The Arabs have their own religious views of Gabriel; these are set forth in the Koran. In Surah II, verses 97 and 98, we read:

"Who is an enemy to Gabriel! For he it is who hath revealed this Scripture to thy heart by Allah's leave, confirming that which was revealed before it, and a guidance and glad tidings to believers; who is an enemy of Allah, and His angels and His messengers, and Gabriel and Michael! Then, lo! Allah Himself is an enemy to the disbelievers."

In the footnote to Surah II, verse 87, we read: "'The

holy Spirit' is a term for the angel of Revelation, Gabriel, on whom be peace.''

Although the Koran in no way connects Gabriel with Noah, it gives reference to both Noah and the flood. For example, Surah III, verse 33, reads: "Lo! Allah preferred Adam and Noah and the Family of Abraham and the Family of Imran above all His creatures.''

Referring to the children of Israel as descendants of Noah and his family, Surah XVII, verse 3, talks of "the seed of those whom We carried in the ship along with Noah.''

The Koran says that the people called Noah a madman, adding, "When the water rose, we carried you upon the ship that we might make it a memorial for you.'' (Surah LI:9.)

Chapter Three

THE CHOSEN SERVANTS

It is inspirational to observe how the Lord chooses and deploys His servants like Noah throughout the centuries for His own divine purposes. Both religious and civic leaders have been thus chosen.

One outstanding such example is that of Cyrus the Great, founder of the Persian empire. Note this comment from the *New Analytical Bible and Dictionary of the Bible:*

"In 538 B.C. he [Cyrus] conquered Babylon. Isaiah names him twice as the divine instrument for the release of the Jews from their Babylonian Exile. (Isa. 44:28; 45: 1-14.) Daniel describes the revelry of Belshazzar and his lords the last night of the empire. (Dan. 5:30-31.) Herodotus states that Cyrus captured Babylon by turning the waters of the Euphrates into an excavation and entered the city by the dry bed of that river, that while the people indulged in a great revelry the gates had been left open.

"Two years after the fall of Babylon, 536 B.C., Cyrus issued a proclamation permitting the Jews to return to their own land. He restored the sacred vessels of the Temple that were carried to Babylon by Nebuchadnezzar. (Ez. 1:1-11; 5:13-14; 6:3.) A large company of Jews responded to this proclamation and returned to Jerusalem under the leadership of Zerubbabel." (Chicago: John A. Dickson Publishing Co., 1941, p. 94.)

Nephi's vision concerning America shows how Christopher Columbus was chosen to discover this continent, leading to its colonization. (See 1 Nephi 13:12-20.) The

coming of the early colonists to America was shown to
Nephi in the same vision, as was the Revolutionary War.
He even saw the outcome of the war. Were not George
Washington and other patriots divinely chosen?

Since America, the choice land of the Lord, was dedicated to freedom, as it was, would not the Lord raise up
the men on whom He would depend to bring about that
freedom? He revealed that He did so as He discussed the
writing of the Constitution of the United States: "And for
this purpose have I established the Constitution of this
land, by the hands of wise men whom I raised up unto this
very purpose, and redeemed the land by the shedding of
blood." (D&C 101:80.)

So America was dedicated to freedom in no uncertain
terms, and the Lord provided the means by which that
freedom was to be maintained. But He gave a stern warning in doing so:

"And the Lord would not suffer that they should stop
beyond the sea in the wilderness, but he would that they
should come forth even unto the land of promise, which
was choice above all other lands, which the Lord God had
preserved for a righteous people.

"And he had sworn in his wrath unto the brother of
Jared, that whoso should possess this land of promise,
from that time henceforth and forever, should serve him,
the true and only God, or they should be swept off when
the fulness of his wrath should come upon them.

"And now, we can behold the decrees of God concerning this land, that it is a land of promise; and whatsoever nation shall possess it shall serve God, or they
shall be swept off when the fulness of his wrath shall come
upon them. And the fulness of his wrath cometh upon
them when they are ripened in iniquity.

"For behold, this is a land which is choice above all
other lands; wherefore he that doth possess it shall serve
God or shall be swept off; for it is the everlasting decree of

God. And it is not until the fulness of iniquity among the children of the land, that they are swept off.

"And this cometh unto you, O ye Gentiles, that ye may know the decrees of God—that ye may repent, and not continue in your iniquities until the fulness come, that ye may not bring down the fulness of the wrath of God upon you as the inhabitants of the land have hitherto done.

"Behold, this is a choice land, and whatsoever nation shall possess it shall be free from bondage, and from captivity, and from all other nations under heaven, if they will but serve the God of the land, who is Jesus Christ, who hath been manifested by the things which we have written." (Ether 2:7-12.)

Inasmuch as liberty was to be the keynote of life in America, could God tolerate slavery on this land? Did He not, then, raise up the great liberator of the slaves, Abraham Lincoln, to cleanse America of this curse? Was not Lincoln a man of God? Was anyone in his day, even in the religious ministry, any more humble or believing than he?

One of the most significant examples of God's planning is shown in the life of Joseph who was sold into Egypt. In his day Palestine did not provide the conditions in which Jacob's family could become a great nation, so the Lord sent them to Egypt, where the land was fertile, where there was a benign government, and where they could grow and prosper. How was it brought about? It was through Joseph's going to Egypt as a slave, but later becoming governor of the nation. It was an act of God. Joseph explained this to his brethren when he made himself known to them as they came for corn. Says the scripture:

"And Joseph said unto his brethren, Come near to me, I pray you. And they came near. And he said, I am Joseph your brother, whom ye sold into Egypt. Now therefore be not grieved, nor angry with yourselves, that ye sold me hither: for God did send me before you to preserve life.

"For these two years hath the famine been in the land: and yet there are five years, in the which there shall neither be earing nor harvest. *And God sent me before you to preserve you a posterity in the earth, and to save your lives by a great deliverance.* So now it was not you that sent me hither, but God: and he hath made me a father to Pharaoh, and the Lord of all his house, and a ruler throughout all the land of Egypt.

"Haste ye, and go up to my father, and say unto him, Thus saith thy son Joseph, God hath made me lord of all Egypt: come down unto me, tarry not; and thou shalt dwell in the land of Goshen, and thou shalt be near unto me, thou, and thy children, and thy children's children, and thy flocks, and thy herds, and all that thou hast: and there will I nourish thee; for yet there are five years of famine; lest thou, and thy household, and all that thou hast, come to poverty." (Genesis 45:4-11.)

The prophet Jeremiah was chosen before he was born. (Jeremiah 1:5.)

The Prophet Joseph Smith said that "every man who has a calling to minister to the inhabitants of the world was ordained to that very purpose in the Grand Council of heaven before the world was. I suppose I was ordained to this very office in that Grand Council." (*History of the Church* 6:364.)

President Joseph Fielding Smith stated an interesting idea when discussing the premortal activities of our great prophets: "It is true that Adam helped to form the earth. He labored with our Savior Jesus Christ. I have a strong view or conviction that there were others also who assisted them. Perhaps Noah and Enoch; and *why not Joseph Smith* and those appointed to be rulers before the earth was formed? We know that Jesus our Savior was a Spirit when this great work was done. He did all of these mighty works before he tabernacled in the flesh.'' (Bruce R. McConkie, comp., *Doctrines of Salvation* 1 [Bookcraft, 1954]: 74-75. Italics in original.)

Obviously our pre-earth life is closely related to our station in mortality. This could apply to all of us, not alone to prophets and kings. Clearly, it related to Noah and his mission with respect to the flood. Noah was Gabriel, the angel-messenger of God. He was second to Adam (Michael) in the eternal world, and he was second to Adam in this world—the second progenitor of man.

Chapter Four

THE DIVINE PATIENCE

There was a long preliminary to the flood and Noah's ministry. Wickedness had been in the earth for generations, during all of which time the Lord had sought earnestly to bring mankind to repentance.

Leading directly to the flood and the work of Noah was the mission of Enoch, also one of the truly great ones, who was sent to earth for a specific purpose. In his day there was a great division among the people. The righteous apparently lived in a land called Canaan, where Enoch was raised. His fathers were "preachers of righteousness, and spake and prophesied, and called upon all men, everywhere, to repent; and faith was taught unto the children of men."

As Enoch journeyed in the land, "the Spirit of God descended out of heaven, and abode upon him.

"And he heard a voice from heaven, saying: Enoch, my son, prophesy unto this people, and say unto them—Repent, for thus saith the Lord: I am angry with this people, and my fierce anger is kindled against them; for their hearts have waxed hard, and their ears are dull of hearing, and their eyes cannot see afar off; and for these many generations, ever since the day that I created them, have they gone astray, and have denied me, and have sought their own counsels in the dark; and in their own abominations have they devised murder, and have not kept the commandments, which I gave unto their father, Adam.

"Wherefore, they have foresworn themselves, and by their oaths, they have brought upon themselves death;

and a hell I have prepared for them, if they repent not.''

Enoch bowed before the Lord and said, "Why is it that I have found favor in thy sight, and am but a lad, and all the people hate me; for I am slow of speech; wherefore am I thy servant?" (Moses 6:23-31.)

Here then is another prophet called in his boyhood, just as Samuel was appointed as a child, and just as Joseph Smith was chosen when he was a boy of but fourteen. Why were these servants thus selected in their childhood? Because God knew them in their premortal life and wanted them while they were unspoiled by worldliness. He could then train them for their special work. As He said to Jeremiah, He could also have said to these three: "Before I formed thee in the belly I knew thee; and before thou camest forth out of the womb I sanctified thee, and I ordained thee a prophet unto the nations." (Jeremiah 1:5.)

Is not God unchangeable? Is He a respecter of persons? He chooses His earthly servants from among those who had served him well in premortality, a most normal procedure.

The Lord comforted Enoch and said: "Go forth and do as I have commanded thee, and no man shall pierce thee. Open thy mouth, and it shall be filled, and I will give thee utterance, for all flesh is in my hands, and I will do as seemeth me good.

"Say unto this people: Choose ye this day, to serve the Lord God who made you. Behold my Spirit is upon you, wherefore all thy words will I justify; and the mountains shall flee before you, and the rivers shall turn from their course; and thou shalt abide in me, and I in you; therefore walk with me."

As part of his preparation, the Lord gave to Enoch a vision of the world and things to come; and based on this vision, Enoch preached details of the gospel to the people. Many came to hear him from far and near, saying, "A seer hath the Lord raised up unto his people." (Moses 6:32-36.)

Enoch declared: "The Lord which spake with me, the same is the God of heaven, and he is my God, and your God, and ye are my brethren, and why counsel ye yourselves, and deny the God of heaven?

"The heavens he made; the earth is his footstool; and the foundation thereof is his. Behold, he laid it, an host of men hath he brought in upon the face thereof. And death hath come upon our fathers; nevertheless we know them, and cannot deny, and even the first of all we know, even Adam. For a book of remembrance we have written among us, according to the pattern given by the finger of God; and it is given in our own language.

"And as Enoch spake forth the words of God, the people trembled, and could not stand in his presence." (Moses 6:43-47.)

The Lord commanded Enoch to ascend a high mountain. Enoch recorded this experience: "I saw the Lord; and he stood before my face, and he talked with me, even as a man talketh one with another, face to face."

The wicked and the righteous of that day were arrayed in battle. As the wicked attacked the people of God, "so great was the faith of Enoch, that he led the people of God, and their enemies came to battle against them; and he spake the word of the Lord, and the earth trembled, and the mountains fled, even according to his command; and the rivers of water were turned out of their course; and the roar of the lions was heard out of the wilderness; and all nations feared greatly, so powerful was the word of Enoch, and so great was the power of the language which God had given him.

"There also came up a land out of the depth of the sea, and so great was the fear of the enemies of the people of God, that they fled and stood afar off and went upon the land which came up out of the depth of the sea.

"And the giants of the land, also, stood afar off; and there went forth a curse upon all people that fought against God; and from that time forth there were wars and bloodshed among them; but the Lord came and dwelt with his people, and they dwelt in righteousness.

"The fear of the Lord was upon all nations, so great was the glory of the Lord, which was upon his people. And the Lord blessed the land, and they were blessed upon the mountains, and upon the high places, and did flourish."

Now comes the first mention of the city of Zion, or the city of Enoch: "And the Lord called his people Zion, because they were of one heart and one mind, and dwelt in righteousness; and there was no poor among them."

Enoch continued his preaching amid great miracles. "And it came to pass in his days, that he built a city that was called the City of Holiness, even Zion. And it came to pass that Enoch talked with the Lord; and he said unto the Lord: Surely Zion shall dwell in safety forever. But the Lord said unto Enoch: Zion have I blessed, but the residue of the people have I cursed."

So righteous were the people of Enoch's city that "Zion, in process of time, was taken up into heaven." (Moses 7.)

Thus there came a separation between the righteous and the wicked. But the Lord left some of His leaders on the earth looking toward the time of the flood. He would continue to appeal to the rebellious to the very last, for He would leave them no excuse.

Of that day President Joseph Fielding Smith wrote:

"Enoch saw in vision the kingdoms of the world and all their inhabitants down even to the end of time. The Lord told him of Noah and the flood and how he would destroy the people of the earth for their iniquity. Of these rebellious ones who rejected the truth and paid no heed to the preachings of Noah and the ancient prophets, the

Lord said: 'I can stretch forth mine hands and hold all the creations which I have made; and mine eye can pierce them also, and among all the workmanship of mine hands there has not been so great wickedness as among thy brethren.

" 'But behold, their sins shall be upon the heads of their fathers; Satan shall be their father, and misery shall be their doom, and the whole heavens shall weep over them, even all the workmanship of mine hands; wherefore should not the heavens weep, seeing these shall suffer? But behold, these which thine eyes are upon shall perish in the floods; and behold, *I will shut them up; a prison have I prepared for them.* And That which I have chosen hath plead before my face. Wherefore, he suffereth for their sins; inasmuch as they will repent *in the day that my Chosen shall return unto me, and until that day they shall be in torment.* (Moses 7:36-39.)' "

President Smith then says: "From this we learn that the Lord has prepared a prison for the souls of all those who rejected the testimony of the antediluvian prophets, where they were to remain in torment *until* the time when Jesus should atone for their sins and return to the Father." (Bruce R. McConkie, comp., *Doctrines of Salvation* 2 [Bookcraft, 1955]: 156-57. Italics in original.)

It is interesting that the city of Enoch will return to the earth. Of this President Smith has said: "In the day of regeneration, when all things are made new, there will be three great cities that will be holy. One will be the Jerusalem of old which shall be rebuilt according to the prophecy of Ezekiel. One will be the city of Zion, or of Enoch, which was taken from the earth when Enoch was translated and which will be restored; and the city Zion, or New Jerusalem, which is to be built by the seed of Joseph on this the American continent."

Then President Smith quotes this scripture:

"And righteousness will I send down out of heaven;

and truth will I send forth out of the earth, to bear testimony of mine Only Begotten; his resurrection from the dead; yea, and also the resurrection of all men; and righteousness and truth will I cause to sweep the earth as with a flood, to gather out mine elect from the four quarters of the earth, unto a place which I shall prepare, an Holy City, that my people may gird up their loins, and be looking forth for the time of my coming; for there shall be my tabernacle, and it shall be called Zion, a New Jerusalem.

"And the Lord said unto Enoch: Then shalt thou and all thy city meet them there, and we will receive them into our bosom, and they shall see us; and we will fall upon their necks, and they shall fall upon our necks, and we will kiss each other;

"And there shall be mine abode, and it shall be Zion, which shall come forth out of all the creations which I have made; and for the space of a thousand years the earth shall rest. (Moses 7:62-64.)" (Joseph Fielding Smith, Jr., comp., *Answers to Gospel Questions* 2 [Deseret Book, 1958]: 105-6.)

Is it harder to accept the flood as a fact than to believe these scriptures regarding the city of Enoch? What a miracle it was when this whole city, with its entire population, was taken into heaven, actually physically lifted off this earth! And what a miracle it will be when that city and all of its inhabitants return!

Which is the greater miracle: covering the earth with water, or the removal of the city of Enoch to heaven and back again?

Chapter Five

A CHILD
OF PROMISE

Noah was a child of promise. The Lord covenanted with Enoch that Noah would come of his (Enoch's) lineage. Methuselah also predicted that Noah would come of his (Methuselah's) family and that all the children of the earth subsequently would be born through Noah and thus be of Methuselah's lineage. He gloried in this and took credit to himself. Says the scripture:

"And all the days of Enoch were four hundred and thirty years. And it came to pass that Methuselah, the son of Enoch, was not taken, that the covenants of the Lord might be fulfilled, which he made to Enoch; for he truly covenanted with Enoch that Noah should be of the fruit of his loins. And it came to pass that Methuselah prophesied that from his loins should spring all the kingdoms of the earth (through Noah), and he took glory unto himself." (Moses 8:1-3.)

In the days of Methuselah a severe famine swept the land, and many died.

Lamech, who was the son of Methuselah, became the father of Noah: "And he called his name Noah, saying: This son shall comfort us concerning our work and toil of our hands, because of the ground which the Lord hath cursed." (Moses 8:9.)

Roman Catholic scholars translate the parallel passages in Genesis like this: "When Lamech was a hundred and eighty-two years old he became the father of a son. He gave him the name of Noah because, he said, 'Here is one who will give us, in the midst of our toil and the laboring of our hands, a consolation derived from the ground that Yahweh cursed.'" (The Jerusalem Bible [Garden City, N.Y.: Doubleday, 1970], Genesis 5:28-29.)

Nothing is known of the childhood of Noah except that when he was ten years old he was ordained to the priesthood under the hands of Methuselah, indicating that he was a faithful child. (D&C 107:52.)

No mention is made of the marriage of Noah. He was 450 years old when Japheth was born. Whether there were any other children during those centuries is not mentioned, although it seems most improbable that there were not.

Forty-two years after Japheth, Shem was born of Japheth's mother. When Noah was 500 years old, Ham was born. "And Noah and his sons hearkened unto the Lord, and gave heed, and they were called the sons of God." (Moses 8:13-15.)

The daughters of Noah's sons, however, were wicked and "sold themselves" to the apostates, the scriptures say.

It should be noted here that Ham, who often is spoken of as an errant one, was fully faithful, and as other references show, he walked with God, as did Noah and the other sons. When Noah and these three sons, and the wives of all four, entered the ark, nothing is said about any children going in with them. Evidently none of their posterity was worthy of being saved from the flood.

Under their divine commission, Noah and his sons preached repentance to the people to the very end, but without results. The Lord, dismayed at the depth of sin in the world, said to Noah: "My Spirit shall not always strive with man, for he shall know that all flesh shall die; yet his days shall be an hundred and twenty years; and if men do not repent, I will send in the floods upon them." (Moses 8:17.)

In his preaching, Noah "taught the things of God, even as it was in the beginning." (Moses 8:16) Evidently he knew the church history of his day. He was the tenth generation from Adam, but the generations overlapped, since everyone apparently lived hundreds of years. No doubt Methuselah, the oldest man, who lived nearly a thousand years, especially kept the memory of the human race and the church well in mind.

There was also revelation, for Noah gave prophecies to the people in his warnings of impending doom. When the Lord said that His Spirit would not always strive with man, he set the conditions of the flood: if the people did not repent in 120 years, the water would come upon them.

There was great contrast between the labors of Enoch and Noah and the results they obtained. Enoch was given tremendous power to do miracles. He could even move mountains. A land arose out of the sea in his day. He rebuked giants, fought off enemies, and converted an entire city to such a point of perfection that it was taken into heaven. Not so with Noah; his mission was different. He would continue with the divine warnings, but he had been chosen especially to survive the flood and begin the human race anew. In his day no longer was it necessary for great miracles to be performed to persuade the people. Matters had gone beyond that point. No record is made of any miracles performed by Noah or his sons. They merely preached to maintain the Lord's warning and to give to any who would receive it the opportunity to repent. But primarily they were assigned to build the ark and make ready for the cleansing of the earth. Then they must repopulate the world after the flood receded.

Chapter Six

THE SONS
OF GOD

Faithful Noah continued to call "upon the children of men that they should repent; but they hearkened not to his words."

The righteous sons of Noah, together with Noah himself, were called the sons of God because of their faithfulness, in contrast to the wicked men about them whom their daughters married in their apostasy. These wicked men now taunted Noah and claimed also to be sons of God, as though to make themselves equal with Noah in the eyes of the people. They jeered at him and said: "Behold, we are the sons of God; have we not taken unto ourselves the daughters of men? And are we not eating and drinking, and marrying and giving in marriage? And our wives bear unto us children, and the same are mighty men, which are like unto men of old, men of great renown. And they hearkened not unto the words of Noah."

The scripture says that "every man was lifted up in the imagination of the thoughts of his heart, being only evil continually."

Noah continued his preaching, but he grieved over the wickedness of the people and their complete refusal to listen to his words. They scorned the idea of a flood. Never had there been such a catastrophe; why should they believe one would come now? They reveled in their sins, their drinking, their feasting, their marriages. They boasted that their children "are mighty men which are like unto men of old, men of great renown."

But Noah "was a just man and perfect in his generation." He had been ordained by the Lord "after his own order," the priesthood after the order of the Son of God (see D&C 84:17-23; 107:64), and he "walked with God, *as did also his three sons,* Shem, Ham, and Japheth." (Moses 8:20-27. Italics added.)

This is significant. Noah's sons walked with God as did their father. No wonder they were called "the sons of God," being so righteous!

As this expression is used in Genesis, however, it is misunderstood. It appears there in this manner: "And it came to pass, when men began to multiply on the face of the earth, and daughters were born unto them, that the sons of God saw the daughters of men that they were fair; and they took them wives of all which they chose." (Genesis 6:1-2.)

The Jerusalem Bible, in a footnote on this passage, says: "The Catholic fathers commonly take the 'sons of God' to be Seth's descendants and the daughters of men those of Cain." But this is not the view of the Latter-day Saints.

The Book of Moses, which was given by revelation both to Moses and Joseph Smith, says: "And Noah and his sons hearkened unto the Lord, and gave heed, and they were called the sons of God. And when these men began to multiply on the face of the earth, and daughters were born unto them, the sons of men saw that those daughters were fair, and they took them wives, even as they chose. And the Lord said unto Noah: The daughters of thy sons have sold themselves; for behold mine anger is kindled against the sons of men, for they will not hearken to my voice." (Moses 8:13-15.)

To understand better the difference between the sons of God and the sons of men, we would do well to read the following: "Now this prophecy Adam spake, as he was moved upon by the Holy Ghost, and a genealogy was kept of the children of God. And this was the book of the generations of Adam, saying: In the day that God created man, in the likeness of God made he him." (Moses 6:8.)

The children of God referred to here are very obviously the believing descendants of Adam, because the book they prepared recorded "the generations of Adam."

To suppose as some do that God came down and consorted with mortal women, and thus developed a new race of "sons of God," is to borrow from the mythology of Greece and Rome. It was therein that the gods from Olympus came down and, by intercourse with the women of the community, raised up "half-gods" or "demigods," as a new race on earth. But it is all mythology, nothing more. Some Bible translations tend to encourage such a theory, however. For example, the following comes from the Jerusalem Bible, a Roman Catholic work, in which Genesis 6:1-4 reads:

"When men had begun to be plentiful on the earth, and daughters had been born to them, the sons of God, looking at the daughters of men, saw that they were pleasing, so they married as many as they chose. Yahweh said, 'My spirit must not for ever be disgraced in man, for he is but flesh; his life shall last no more than a hundred and twenty years.' The Nephilim were on the earth at that time (and even afterward) when the sons of God resorted to the daughters of man, and had children by them. These are the heroes of days gone by, the famous men."

When that text refers to these offspring as being "the heroes of days gone by, the famous men," it seems to set them apart as some special and superior type of beings, possibly not merely human, but better.

A Bible dictionary says that the Nephilim referred to in this passage were giant demigods who lived in those days. (*New Analytical Bible and Dictionary of the Bible.*) Enoch spoke of them as a depraved lot who sought to murder him. *But part divine and part human they were not,* for God at no time consorted with the "daughters of men." It is sacrilege even to mention such a thing.

Also damaging and misleading are some of the other translations of the Bible on this point. Note, for example, this passage from the Moffatt Translation: "Now when men began to multiply over all the world and had daughters born to them, the angels noticed that the daughters of men were beautiful, and they married any one of them that they chose." This at least removed the idea that the Deity had mingled with mortal women. But did even the angels?

Note this further divergent view from the *American Translation* by Smith and Goodspeed: "The sons of the Gods noticed that the daughters of men were attractive, so they married those whom they liked best. . . . There were giants on the earth who were born to the sons of the Gods whenever they had intercourse with the daughters of men; these were the heroes who were men of note in the days of old."

The Roman Catholic Knox Translation also gives the idea that two kinds of people were on earth, the descendants of men and the descendants of God: "Time passed, and the race of men began to spread over the face of the earth, they and the daughters that were born to them. And now the sons of God saw how beautiful were these daughters of men, and took them as wives. . . . Giants lived on the earth in those days, when first the sons of God mated with the daughters of men, and by them had children; these were the heroes whose fame has come down to us from long ago." (Genesis 6:1-4.)

It is incredible how far afield these translators, supposedly great scholars, could stray. The "sons of gods mating with the daughters of men" indeed! There was no such mating as these passages indicate because there were not two different races there.

Thank heaven for the Prophet Joseph Smith and his sensible and correct rendering of these passages, which he gave by inspiration: "And Noah and his sons hearkened

unto the Lord, and gave heed; and they were called the
sons of God. And when these men began to multiply on
the face of the earth, and daughters were born unto them,
the sons of men saw that their daughters were fair, and
they took them wives even as they chose." (Joseph Smith
Translation, Genesis 8:1-2.)

There was only one human race. All were descendants
of Adam. Those who were righteous were called the children or sons of God, and those who were wicked were
called the sons of men. It was righteousness and wickedness that drew the line of demarcation, not descent from
two sources.

When the apostle Paul preached from Mars Hill in
Athens, the very heartland of Greek mythology, he fought
this demigod theory. As he explained the truth about "the
unknown God," he declared that God "hath made of *one
blood all nations of men* for to dwell on all the face of the
earth, and hath determined the times before appointed
and the bounds of their habitation." (Acts 17:26. Italics
added.)

The Nephilim were described as giants—how big we
do not know. Were they like Goliath? In any case, the
giants who lived in Enoch's day were a depraved lot who
sought to murder him. But part divine and part human
they were not, for neither God, angels, nor "the sons
of the gods" consorted with earthly women as implied.

Certain persons try to use Luke 3:38 to sustain their
mistaken point. The King James Version reads: "Which
was the son of Enos, which was the son of Seth, which
was the son of Adam, which was the son of God." (Luke
3:38.) But when the Prophet Joseph revised the scriptures, he changed that and made it read: "And of Enos,
and of Seth, and of Adam, who was formed of God, and
the first man upon the earth." (JST, Luke 3:45.) This
harmonizes with the Genesis doctrine and other references to the origin of Adam.

In the correct sense Moses also declared as he confronted Satan: "Who art thou? For behold, I am a son of God, in the similitude of his Only Begotten; and where is thy glory, that I should worship thee?" (Moses 1:13.)

It is also well to read Moses 7:1, wherein all believers are designated as the children of God: "And it came to pass that Enoch continued his speech, saying: Behold, our father Adam taught these things, and many have believed and become the sons of God, and many have believed not, and have perished in their sins, and are looking forth with fear, in torment, for the fiery indignation of the wrath of God to be poured out upon them." (Moses 7:1.)

The term was applied directly to Noah and his sons: "And Noah and his sons hearkened unto the Lord, and gave heed, and they were called the sons of God." (Moses 8:13.)

It is obvious, then, that as men became converted to Christ, they were called the sons of God.

There is still further evidence of this fact. John the apostle spoke of the believers: "Beloved, now are we the sons of God, and it doth not yet appear what we shall be: but we know that, when he shall appear, we shall be like him; for we shall see him as he is." (1 John 3:2.)

King Benjamin told his believing followers: "And now, because of the covenant which ye have made ye shall be called the children of Christ, his sons, and his daughters; for behold, this day he hath spiritually begotten you; for ye say that your hearts are changed through faith on his name; therefore, ye are born of him and have become his sons and his daughters." (Mosiah 5:7.)

Moroni said this: "Wherefore, I beseech of you, brethren, that ye should search diligently in the light of Christ that ye may know good from evil; and if ye will lay hold upon every good thing, and condemn it not, ye certainly will be a child of Christ."(Moroni 7:19.)

And the Lord Himself said to the Prophet Joseph: "Hearken unto the voice of the Lord your God, while I speak unto you, Emma Smith, my daughter; for verily I say unto you, all those who receive my gospel are sons and daughters in my kingdom." (D&C 25:1.)

The Lord also said: "Who so loved the world that he gave his own life, that as many as would believe might become the sons of God. Wherefore you are my son; and blessed are you because you have believed." (D&C 34:3-4.)

Of course, any who suppose that God had children in the flesh, as suggested by the false worldly theories, would do well to remember that Jesus Christ of Nazareth is the Only Begotten Son of God, as is repeated so often in the scripture. That alone should settle the matter.

Chapter Seven

THE
FOREWARNINGS

Ample forewarning was given by the Lord concerning the destructive flood that would be sent if the people failed to repent. Actually it was given over a period of four generations, and they were generations of hundreds of years each.

Modern scripture joins with the Bible in describing the long-suffering and patience of the Lord as he tried in every way to bring his children back from their waywardness. Those who doubt that there was a flood must admit that it is mentioned repeatedly in holy writ. To doubt the flood is to question the scriptures that tell of it.

Jesus Christ was the God of the Old Testament. It was He who spoke to the prophets. He gave instruction to Moses. What we call the Book of Moses was given by revelation to Moses, and was similarly given by revelation to the Prophet Joseph Smith. And that book discusses Noah and the flood in great detail.

Neither of these prophets lived at the time of the flood. Their information could come only by revelation. Both communed with Christ Himself.

When Jesus was on earth and foretold the time of his second coming, he did not hesitate to verify the account of Noah and the flood. He actually described conditions at the time of his coming in terms of Noah's day. He said: "But as the days of Noe were, so shall also the coming of the Son of man be. For as in the days that were before the flood they were eating and drinking, marrying and giving in marriage, until the day that Noe entered into the ark." (Matthew 24:37-38.)

Luke's version is certainly to the point: "And as it was in the days of Noe, so shall it be also in the days of the Son of man. They did eat, they drank, they married wives, they were given in marriage, until the day that Noe entered into the ark, and the flood came, and destroyed them all." (Luke 17:26-27.)

Is there any misunderstanding those words?

Isaiah also bore testimony to the facts in the matter. Was it not Jesus who said, "Great are the words of Isaiah"? (3 Nephi 23:1.) That prophet said: "For this is as the waters of Noah unto me: for as I have sworn that the waters of Noah should no more go over the earth; so have I sworn that I would not be wroth with thee, nor rebuke thee." (Isaiah 54:9.)

And the Apostle Paul was not silent either. He declared: "By faith Noah, being warned of God of things not seen as yet, moved with fear, prepared an ark to the saving of his house; by the which he condemned the world, and became heir of the righteousness which is by faith." (Hebrews 11:7.)

This is a great assertion of the fact of Noah's mission. Paul was lecturing on faith, and he cited as outstanding examples the works of Abraham, Isaac, and Jacob. He told also of those who died for the faith, of those who conquered Jericho, of those "who through faith subdued kingdoms, wrought righteousness, obtained promises, stopped the mouths of lions, quenched the violence of fire, escaped the edge of the sword, out of weakness were made strong, waxed valiant in fight, turned to flight the armies of the aliens.

"Women received their dead raised to life again: and others were tortured, not accepting deliverance; that they might obtain a better resurrection: And others had trial of cruel mockings and scourgings, yea, moreover of bonds and imprisonment: They were stoned, they were sawn asunder, were tempted, were slain with the sword: they

wandered about in sheepskins and goatskins; being desti-
tute, afflicted, tormented." (Hebrews 11:33-37.)

One of Paul's prime examples was Noah, for by faith
in this same God of Abraham, Isaac, and Jacob, Noah
"prepared the ark to the saving of his house."

This chapter in Hebrews lends special certainty to the
facts of our religion, to the existence of God, and to the
willingness of many even to die for the faith. If we believe
scripture at all, we certainly believe in the Apostle Paul
and his inspired writings. Will we not believe what he says
about Noah and the ark? To reject the words of Paul is to
defy him and his work.

When the Lord spoke to Enoch, He predicted the
flood in no uncertain terms:

"And the fire of mine indignation is kindled against
them; and in my hot displeasure will I send in the floods
upon them, for my fierce anger is kindled against them.
Behold, I am God; Man of Holiness is my name; Man of
Counsel is my name; and Endless and Eternal is my
name, also. Wherefore, I can stretch forth mine hands and
hold all the creations which I have made; and mine eye
can pierce them also, and among all the workmanship of
mine hands there has not been so great wickedness as
among thy brethren.

"But behold, their sins shall be upon the heads of their
fathers; Satan shall be their father, and misery shall be
their doom; and the whole heavens shall weep over them,
even all the workmanship of mine hands; wherefore
should not the heavens weep, seeing these shall suffer?
But behold, these which thine eyes are upon shall perish
in the floods, and behold, I will shut them up; a prison
have I prepared for them." (Moses 7:34-38.)

One of the most interesting passages relating to the
flood occurs in the book of Ether in the Book of Mormon.
Moroni, who abridged the writings of Ether, tells the story
of the brother of Jared, who conversed with the Lord at

the time of the tower of Babel, following the flood. The Book of Mormon account is evidence of the fact of Noah's ministry, the salvation of the family of Jared, their developing into a numerous people, and their being spared the confusion of their language at the tower. The Jaredites were brought to the land that was "choice above all other lands," the land of America. Note that it was *after* the flood that the land was designated as "choice above all other lands." The book of Ether states:

"And now I, Moroni, proceed to finish my record concerning the destruction of the people of whom I have been writing. For behold, they rejected all the words of Ether; for he truly told them of all things, from the beginning of man; and that after the waters had receded from off the face of this land it became a choice land above all other lands, a chosen land of the Lord; wherefore the Lord would have that all men should serve him who dwell upon the face thereof; and that it was the place of the New Jerusalem, which should come down out of heaven, and the holy sanctuary of the Lord.

"Behold, Ether saw the days of Christ, and he spake concerning a New Jerusalem upon this land. And he spake also concerning the house of Israel, and the Jerusalem from whence Lehi should come—after it should be destroyed it should be built up again, a holy city unto the Lord; wherefore, it could not be a new Jerusalem for it had been in a time of old; but it should be built up again, and become a holy city of the Lord; and it should be built unto the house of Israel—and that a New Jerusalem should be built upon this land, unto the remnant of the seed of Joseph, for which things there has been a type.

"For as Joseph brought his father down into the land of Egypt, even so he died there; wherefore, the Lord brought a remnant of the seed of Joseph out of the land of Jerusalem, that he might be merciful unto the seed of

Joseph that they should perish not, even as he was merciful unto the father of Joseph that he should perish not.

"Wherefore, the remnant of the house of Joseph shall be built upon this land; and it shall be a land of their inheritance; and they shall build up a holy city unto the Lord, like unto the Jerusalem of old; and they shall no more be confounded, until the end come when the earth shall pass away." (Ether 13:1-8.)

It is remarkable! After the flood had receded from the face of the land, it became a choice land above all other lands, a chosen land of the Lord. Indeed, this is something to ponder on. Is this not proof that the flood was a reality, and that out of that flood came America? Out of that flood came the "chosen land of the Lord." Shall we acknowledge it? It is one of the great facts concerning our dispensation!

From the days of Noah, America was dedicated to one great purpose: "Wherefore the Lord would have that all men should serve him who dwell upon the face thereof." (Ether 13:2.)

The land must have been choice prior to the flood also, for it was the home of God's ancient people, the Garden of Eden. In the creation it was pronounced "good" and "very good." The Garden of Eden, we know from the teachings of the Prophet Joseph Smith, is in the region of Jackson County, Missouri.

Could it be that in the flood the Lord cleansed that land of its wickedness because even then it was choice in His sight? Did he determine that the area of the Garden of Eden should suffer no more corruption? Has the decree carried over from then to now, that people who live in America must serve God or be swept off the land?

It is still the same land, the same region. The command is still the same: the Almighty will sweep off any nation that occupies the land and refuses to serve the God of the land, who is Jesus Christ.

Could the same requirement have applied before the flood as well as afterward? Was it from what is now America that the ark was floated? It landed halfway around the world on Mt. Ararat, in what is today eastern Turkey, leaving the choicest of all lands far behind.

Chapter Eight

THE SCRIPTURAL PROOF

People who question whether there ever was a flood or an ark, or even whether Noah lived, come face to face with direct revelation. Modern scripture sustains the flood story. Modern scripture affirms the existence of Noah, the wickedness of the people of his day, and the determination of the Lord to wash the earth clean with a deluge.

Consider the Book of Moses in the Pearl of Great Price. It was revelation from God to Moses in Moses' day, and it was repeated as revelation from God to Joseph Smith in our day, in June 1830. To reject Noah and the flood, then, would be a rejection of the revealed word of God!

Note how the Book of Moses begins: "The words of God, which he spake unto Moses at a time when Moses was caught up into an exceedingly high mountain.

"And he saw God face to face, and he talked with him, and the glory of God was upon Moses; therefore Moses could endure his presence.

"And God spake unto Moses, saying: Behold, I am the Lord God Almighty, and Endless is my name; for I am without beginning of days or end of years; and is not this endless?

"And, behold, thou art my son; wherefore look, and I will show thee the workmanship of mine hands; but not all, for my works are without end, and also my words, for they never cease.

"Wherefore, no man can behold all my works, except he behold all my glory; and no man can behold all my glory, and afterwards remain in the flesh on the earth."

Then comes the divine call to Moses: "And I have a work for thee, Moses, my son; and thou art in the similitude of mine Only Begotten; and mine Only Begotten is and shall be the Savior, for he is full of grace and truth; but there is no God beside me, and all things are present with me, for I know them all." (Moses 1:3-6.)

Now begins the vision of Moses as he and the Almighty discussed creation:

"And now, behold, this one thing I show unto thee, Moses, my son; for thou art in the world, and now I show it unto thee.

"And it came to pass that Moses looked, and beheld the world upon which he was created; and Moses beheld the world and the ends thereof, and all the children of men which are, and which were created; of the same he greatly marveled and wondered. . . .

"And behold, the glory of the Lord was upon Moses, so that Moses stood in the presence of God, and talked with him face to face. And the Lord God said unto Moses: For mine own purpose have I made these things. Here is wisdom and it remaineth in me. And by the word of my power, have I created them, which is mine Only Begotten Son, who is full of grace and truth. And worlds without number have I created; and I also created them for mine own purpose; and by the Son I created them, which is mine Only Begotten." (Moses 1:7-8, 31-33.)

Do we accept God as the Creator? Do we believe that Jesus Christ is the Only Begotten Son of God? The Lord here affirms it!

Part of the divine affirmation regarding Creation and His Only Begotten Son is the text of the revelation that follows, establishing the fact of the existence of Enoch and his city; of Methuselah, the oldest man; and of Methuselah's grandson, Noah.

To reject Noah, are we also to reject Enoch and his city? God made a covenant with Enoch that Noah would be born in his (Enoch's) lineage. Do we reject that account? Was not Enoch one of the greatest prophets? Does not modern revelation declare that he and his city will return to earth incident to the second coming of Christ? Then was not Enoch a real person? Did he not walk and talk with God? Then did he not covenant with God, and was that covenant not divinely accepted? Was the covenant not a fact?

The covenant bound the Lord to send Noah into the family of Enoch, as Enoch's great-grandson. (Moses 8:2.) Not only was Enoch promised that Noah would be one of his descendants, but also the Lord told him about the flood. Then can we doubt it?

The Lord gave mighty visions to Enoch, including a view of the wicked who would die in the flood. The sacred record reads: "But behold, these which thine eyes are upon shall perish in the floods; and behold, I will shut them up; a prison have I prepared for them." (Moses 7:38.) Then did the wicked not die in the flood? Could they have done so if there was no flood?

Notice the reference in that verse to the prison house to which these wicked ones would be taken following their drowning: Where is another reference to this same prison?

One of our best-known Bible passages tells of Christ's visit to these identical spirits while His body lay in the tomb following His crucifixion:

"For Christ also hath once suffered for sins, the just for the unjust, that he might bring us to God, being put to death in the flesh, but quickened by the Spirit: By which also he went and preached unto the spirits in prison; which sometime were disobedient, when once the long-suffering of God waited in the days of Noah, while the ark was a preparing, wherein few, that is, eight souls were saved by water." (1 Peter 3:18-20.)

In that connection Peter also said: "For for this cause

was the gospel preached also to them that are dead, that they might be judged according to men in the flesh, but live according to God in the spirit." (1 Peter 4:6.)

The doctrine of salvation for the dead thus becomes a testimony to the reality of Noah and the flood.

Enoch was shown more: "And Enoch also saw Noah, and his family; that the posterity of all the sons of Noah should be saved with a temporal salvation; wherefore Enoch saw that Noah built an ark; and that the Lord smiled upon it, and held it in his own hand; but upon the residue of the wicked the floods came and swallowed them up." (Moses 7:42-43.)

So the Lord showed Enoch both Noah and his ark. Can we deny that it affirms the earlier declaration of the Lord, who said to Enoch, "Behold these thy brethren; they are the workmanship of mine own hands, and I gave unto them their knowledge, in the day I created them; and in the Garden of Eden, gave I unto man his agency; and unto thy brethren have I said, and also given commandment, that they should love one another, and that they should choose me, their Father; but behold, they are without affection, and they hate their own blood; and the fire of mine indignation is kindled against them; and in my hot displeasure will I send in the floods upon them, for my fierce anger is kindled against them." (Moses 7:32-34.)

"And it came to pass that Enoch continued his cry unto the Lord, saying: I ask thee, O Lord, in the name of thine Only Begotten, even Jesus Christ, that thou wilt have mercy upon Noah and his seed, that the earth might never more be covered by the floods.

"And the Lord could not withhold; and he covenanted with Enoch, and sware unto him with an oath, that he would stay the floods; that he would call upon the children of Noah; and he sent forth an unalterable decree, that a remnant of his seed should always be found among all nations, while the earth should stand;

"And the Lord said: Blessed is he through whose seed Messiah shall come; for he saith—I am Messiah, the King of Zion, the Rock of Heaven, which is broad as eternity; whoso cometh in at the gate and climbeth up by me shall never fall; wherefore, blessed are they of whom I have spoken, for they shall come forth with songs of everlasting joy." (Moses 7:50-53.)

The Lord in His mercy—in His great desire to save His children—agreed to stay the floods for 120 years to give Noah further opportunity to bring man to repentance.

"And it came to pass that Noah prophesied, and taught the things of God, even as it was in the beginning.

"And the Lord said unto Noah: My Spirit shall not always strive with man, for he shall know that all flesh shall die; yet his days shall be an hundred and twenty years; and if men do not repent, I will send in the floods upon them.

"And it came to pass that Noah called upon the children of men that they should repent; but they hearkened not unto his words. And it repented Noah, and his heart was pained that the Lord had made man on the earth, and it grieved him at the heart.

"And the Lord said: I will destroy man whom I have created, from the face of the earth, both man and beast, and the creeping things, and the fowls of the air; for it repenteth Noah that I have created them, and that I have made them; and he hath called upon me; for they have sought his life.

"And thus Noah found grace in the eyes of the Lord; for Noah was a just man, and perfect in his generation; and he walked with God, as did also his three sons, Shem, Ham, and Japheth.

"The earth was corrupt before God, and it was filled with violence. And God looked upon the earth, and, behold, it was corrupt, for all flesh had corrupted its way upon the earth. And God said unto Noah: The end of all flesh is come before me, for the earth is filled with violence, and behold I will destroy all flesh from off the earth." (Moses 8:16-17, 20, 25-30.)

And so the floods came. This is modern revelation to the Prophet Joseph Smith, comparable to the revelations in the Doctrine and Covenants. The reality of Noah is fully affirmed in other scripture also. Note what is said about his priesthood:

"Abraham received the priesthood from Melchizedek, who received it through the lineage of his fathers, even till Noah; and from Noah till Enoch, through the lineage of their fathers; and from Enoch to Abel, who was slain by the conspiracy of his brother, who received the priesthood by the commandments of God, by the hand of his father Adam, who was the first man—Which priesthood continueth in the church of God in all generations, and is without beginning of days or end of years." (D&C 84:14-17.)

Note that Methuselah ordained him: "Noah was ten years old when he was ordained under the hand of Methuselah." (D&C 107:52.)

When the Savior comes, He will gather His redeemed about Him, and one of them will be Noah. Then did Noah live? And did he minister for the Lord? Through Joseph Smith we have this assurance:

"And now the year of my redeemed is come; and they shall mention the loving kindness of their Lord, and all that he has bestowed upon them according to his goodness, and according to his loving kindness, forever and ever.

"In all their afflictions he was afflicted. And the angel of his presence saved them; and in his love, and in his pity, he redeemed them, and bore them, and carried them all the days of old; yea, and Enoch also, and they who were with him; the prophets who were before him; and Noah also, and they who were before him; and Moses also, and they who were before him; and from Moses to Elijah, and from Elijah to John, who were with Christ in his resurrection, and the holy apostles, with Abraham, Isaac, and Jacob, shall be in the presence of the Lamb.

"And the graves of the saints shall be opened; and they shall come forth and stand on the right hand of the Lamb, when he shall stand upon Mount Zion, and upon the holy city, the New Jerusalem; and they shall sing the song of the Lamb, day and night forever and ever." (D&C 133:52-56.)

Chapter Nine

THE FLOOD
CAME

As predicted, the floods came, the ark was launched, and Noah and his wife, his sons and their wives—but none of their children—floated in safety.

Many have tried to explain that there was not enough water on earth to make the flood; others say that the mountains could not possibly have been covered. Some say the flood was strictly a local tragedy covering only a small area of the earth.

We do not argue with scientists or scholars over their defensive views. We tell the story of scripture, and scripture is the word of God, verified by modern revelation over and over again.

Since the King James Version of the Bible is so readily available, and the story of the flood is told there so clearly, as a matter of interest we quote from other translations. The Jerusalem Bible records some of the facts in a slightly different manner. In the sixth and seventh chapters of Genesis in that version of the Bible we read:

"Yahweh saw that the wickedness of man was great on the earth, and that the thoughts in his heart fashioned nothing but wickedness all day long. Yahweh regretted having made man on the earth, and his heart grieved. 'I will rid the earth's face of man, my own creations,' Yahweh said, 'and of animals also, reptiles too, and the birds of heaven; for I regret having made them.' But Noah had found favour with Yahweh.

"This is the story of Noah:

"Noah was a good man, a man of integrity among his contemporaries, and he walked with God. Noah became the father of three sons, Shem, Ham and Japheth. The earth grew corrupt in God's sight, and filled with violence. God contemplated the earth; it was corrupt, for corrupt were the ways of all flesh on the earth.

"God said to Noah, 'The end has come for all things of flesh; I have decided this, because the earth is full of violence of man's making, and I will efface them from the earth. Make yourself an ark out of resinous wood. Make it with reeds and line it with pitch inside and out. This is how to make it: the length of the ark is to be three hundred cubits, its breadth fifty cubits, and its height thirty cubits. Make a roof for the ark . . . put the door of the ark high up in the side, and make a first, second and third deck.

" 'For my part I mean to bring a flood, and send the waters over the earth, to destroy all flesh on it, every living creature under heaven; everything on earth shall perish. But I will establish my Covenant with you, and you must go on board the ark, yourself, your sons, your wife, and your sons' wives along with you. From all living creatures, from all flesh, you must take two of each kind aboard the ark, to save their lives with yours; they must be a male and a female. Of every kind of bird, of every kind of animal and of every kind of reptile on the ground, two must go with you so that their lives may be saved. For your part provide yourself with eatables of all kinds, and lay in a store of them, to serve as food for yourself and them.' Noah did this; he did all that God had ordered him.

"Yahweh said to Noah, 'Go aboard the ark, you and all your household, for you alone among this generation do I see as a good man in my judgment. Of all the clean animals you must take seven of each kind, both male and female; of the unclean animals you must take two, a male and its female (and of the birds of heaven also, seven of each kind, both male and female), to propagate their kind over the whole earth. For in seven days' time I mean to make it rain on the earth for forty days and nights, and I

will rid the earth of every living thing that I made.' Noah
did all that Yahweh ordered.

"Noah was six hundred years old when the flood of
waters appeared on the earth.

"Noah with his sons, his wife, and his sons' wives
boarded the ark to escape the waters of the flood. (Of the
clean animals and the animals that are not clean, of the
birds and all that crawls on the ground, two of each kind
boarded the ark with Noah, a male and a female, according to the order God gave Noah.) Seven days later the
waters of the flood appeared on the earth.

"In the six hundredth year of Noah's life, in the second month, and on the seventeenth day of that month,
that very day all the springs of the great deep broke
through, and the sluices of heaven opened. It rained on
the earth for forty days and forty nights.

"That very day Noah and his sons Shem, Ham and
Japheth boarded the ark, with Noah's wife and the three
wives of his sons, and with them wild beasts of every
kind, cattle of every kind, reptiles of every kind that
crawls on the earth, birds of every kind, all that flies,
everything with wings. One pair of all that is flesh and has
the breath of life boarded the ark with Noah; and so there
went in a male and a female of every creature that is flesh,
just as God had ordered him.

"And Yahweh closed the door behind Noah.

"The flood lasted forty days on the earth. The waters
swelled, lifting the ark until it was raised above the earth.
The waters rose and swelled greatly on the earth. After a
hundred and fifty days the waters fell, and in the seventh
month, the earth so that all the highest mountains under
the whole of heaven were submerged. The waters rose
fifteen cubits higher, submerging the mountains. And so
all things of flesh perished that moved on the earth, birds,
cattle, wild beasts, everything that swarms on the earth,
and every man. Everything with the breath of life in its

nostrils died, everything on dry land. Yahweh destroyed every living thing on the face of the earth, man and animals, reptiles, and the birds of heaven. He rid the earth of them, so that only Noah was left, and those with him in the ark. The waters rose on the earth for a hundred and fifty days.''

No mention is made that human beings lived in all parts of the earth. Seemingly they lived in communities in one general area, as in the days of Enoch. But that is not to say that the whole planet was not covered with water in the flood. The record says the whole earth, ''all under the whole of heaven,'' was submerged.

Chapter Ten

FACTS CONFIRMED

All Bible translations give essentially the same account of the flood and the manner by which it came about. It is interesting to note that the fountains of the earth gushed forth, adding to the floods. It was not rain alone, although the heavens "wept" for forty days.

The Knox Translation of the Bible reads: "God wiped out the whole world of earthly creatures, man and beast, creeping things and all that flies through the air, so that they vanished from the earth; only Noe and his companions in the Ark were left. And the waters held their own over the land for a hundred and fifty days."

The Revised Standard Version reads: "The waters prevailed and increased greatly upon the earth . . . and the waters prevailed so mightily upon the earth that all the high mountains under the whole heaven were covered. . . . And all flesh died that moved upon the earth, birds, cattle, beasts, all swarming creatures that swarm upon the earth, and every man. . . . He blotted out every living thing that was upon the face of the ground, man and animals and creeping things and birds of the air; they were blotted out from the earth. Only Noah was left, and those that were with him in the ark." (Genesis 7:18-23.)

The New World Translation expresses it this way: "And the waters overwhelmed the earth so greatly that all the tall mountains that were under the whole heaven came to be covered. Up to fifteen cubits the waters overwhelmed them and the mountains became covered." (Genesis 7:19-20.)

The Moffatt Translation says: "The fountains of the

great abyss all burst, and the sluices of heaven were opened. . . . the waters swelled mightily on the earth, till every high mountain under heaven was covered—the waters swelling twenty-two feet higher, till the mountains were covered, and every living creature perished." (Genesis 7:12, 18-21.)

The Prophet Joseph Smith's translation states: "And the waters prevailed exceedingly upon the face of the earth, and all the high hills, under the whole heavens were covered. Fifteen cubits and upward did the waters prevail; and the mountains were covered." (JST, Genesis 8:41.)

The Jerusalem Bible reads: "But God had Noah in mind, and all the wild beasts and all the cattle that were with him in the ark. God sent a wind across the earth and the waters subsided. The springs of the deep and the sluices of heaven were stopped. Rain ceased to fall from heaven; the waters gradually ebbed from the earth. After a hundred and fifty days the waters fell, and in the seventh month, on the seventeenth day of that month, the ark came to rest on the mountains of Ararat. The waters gradually fell until the tenth month when, on the first day of the tenth month, the mountain peaks appeared.

"At the end of forty days Noah opened the porthole he had made in the ark and he sent out the raven. This went off, and flew back and forth until the waters dried up from the earth. Then he sent out the dove, to see whether the waters were receding from the surface of the earth. The dove, finding nowhere to perch, returned to him in the ark, for there was water over the whole surface of the earth; putting out his hand he took hold of it and brought it back into the ark with him. After waiting seven more days, again he sent out the dove from the ark. In the evening, the dove came back to him and there it was with a new olive branch in its beak. So Noah realized that the waters were receding from the earth. After waiting seven more days he sent out the dove, and now it returned to him no more.

"It was in the six hundred and first year of Noah's life, in the first month and on the first of the month, that the water dried up from the earth. Noah lifted back the hatch of the ark and looked out. The surface of the ground was dry!

"In the second month and on the twenty-seventh day of the month the earth was dry." (Genesis 8:1-14.)

Note a dictionary comment:

"Noah left the ark on the twenty-seventh day of the second month (Genesis 8:14-19) so that the duration of the Deluge was twelve lunar months and ten days, or one solar year.

"As to the extent of the flood one opinion is that it was general, over the whole earth, another that it covered only those regions inhabited by man. The view that it was limited to a certain section is supported by the design of the flood, i.e., to destroy the race which must have been confined within a certain area. Noah could not have preached righteousness to people in all parts of the world, and it would have been necessary for the ark to contain a far greater number of animals than would have been possible by the dimensions given. It was 'universal' only as it affected the whole race at that time.

"The many notices of the flood in Babylonian, Syrian, Armenian, Persian, Chinese and other traditions, clearly indicate that the facts had been carried down to the descendants of Ham, Shem, and Japheth, which could have been done for centuries by those who passed through the flood. Noah lived for three hundred and fifty years after the flood. (Genesis 9:28-29.)" (*The New Analytical Bible and Dictionary of the Bible,* p. 121.)

These, of course, are but the deductions of men, human wisdom attempting to explain the mysteries of God, an impossibility. We are in no sense bound by them.

Chapter Eleven

DETAILED PREPARATION

The Lord was most specific in giving His preparatory instructions to Noah. Not only did He prescribe the rules for constructing the ark, but He also outlined with care what Noah was to do about the animals. He said:

"Thou shalt come into the ark, thou and thy sons, and thy wife, and thy sons' wives with them. And of every living thing of all flesh, two of every kind shalt thou bring into the ark, to keep alive with thee; they shall be male and female. Of fowls after their kind, and of cattle after their kind, of every creeping thing of the earth after his kind; two of every kind shalt thou take into the ark, to keep alive.

"And take thou unto thee of all food that is eaten, and thou shalt gather fruit of every kind unto thee in the ark, and it shall be for food for thee, and for them.

"Thus did Noah, according to all that God commanded him. And the Lord said unto Noah, Come thou and all thy house, into the ark; for thee only have I seen righteous before me, in the generation. Of every clean beast thou shalt take to thee by sevens, the male and his female; and of beasts that are not clean by two, the male and his female; of fowls also of the air, by sevens, the male and his female; to keep seed alive upon the face of the earth." (JST, Genesis 8:24-31.)

Note that reference is made to the food Noah and his family would eat and also the food for the animals in the ark. Note also that of the clean beasts Noah took into the ark seven and seven, whereas of the unclean he took only two and two. This would permit him to offer burnt offerings to the Lord as soon as the flood subsided, without interfering with the procreation of life to replenish the earth.

The Lord also made a covenant with Noah before the flood came, saying: "With thee I will establish my covenant, even as I have sworn unto thy father, Enoch, that of thy posterity shall come all nations." (JST, Genesis 8:23; Moses 7:50-52.) This was divine assurance that indeed Noah would become the father of all human beings from then on.

For 150 days the ark floated, and finally it came to rest on Mount Ararat in what was formerly Armenia and is now Turkey.

Josephus, in his *Antiquities,* gives this sidelight:

"When the rain ceased, the water did but just begin to abate, after one hundred and fifty days (that is, on the seventeenth day of the seventh month) it then ceased to subside for a little while.

"After this the ark rested on the top of a certain mountain in Armenia; which, when Noah understood, he opened it; and seeing a small piece of land about it, he continued quiet, and conceived some cheerful hopes of deliverance; but a few days afterward, when the water was decreased to a greater degree, he sent out a raven, as desirous to learn whether any other part of the earth were left dry by the water, and whether he might go out of the ark with safety; but the raven, finding all the land still overflowed, returned to Noah again.

"And after seven days he sent out a dove, to know the state of the ground; which came back to him covered with mud, and bringing an olive branch. Hereby Noah learned that the earth was become clear of the flood.

"So after he had stayed seven more days, he sent the living creatures out of the ark; and both he and his family went out, when he also sacrificed to God, and feasted with his companions. However, the Armenians call this place

The Place of Descent; for the ark being saved in that place, its remains are shewn there by the inhabitants to this day.

"Now all the writers of Barbarian histories make mention of this flood and of this ark; among whom is Berosus the Chaldean; for when he is describing the circumstances of the flood, he goes on thus:—'It is said there is still some part of this ship in Armenia, at the mountain of Cordyaeans; and that some people carry off pieces of the bitumen, which they take away, and use chiefly as amulets for the averting of mischiefs.' Hieronymus the Egyptian, also, who wrote the Phoenician Antiquities, and Mnaseas, and a great many more, make mention of the same. Nay, Nicolaus of Damascus, in his ninety-sixth book, hath a particular relation about them, where he speaks thus:—'There is a great mountain in Armenia, over Minyas, called Baris, upon which it is reported that many who fled at the time of the Deluge were saved; and that one who was carried in an ark came on shore upon the top of it; and that the remains of the timber were a great while preserved.''

THE DELUGE: A BAPTISM

When the scholars made their explanatory notes in the Jerusalem Bible concerning the flood, they related the deluge to a baptism. They said that "Noah's salvation pre-figures the saving waters of baptism." Their interpretation is interesting, inasmuch as our own leaders said a similar thing. President Joseph Fielding Smith wrote:

"Now a word as to the reason for the flood. *It was the baptism of the earth, and that had to be by immersion.* If the water did not cover the entire earth, then it was not baptized, for the baptism of the Lord is not pouring or sprinkling. These forms are strictly man made and not a part of the gospel ordinances." (*Doctrines of Salvation* 2:320.)

President Smith then quoted from the teachings of some of the presidents and apostles of the Church, including the following:

President Brigham Young: "It [the earth] has already had a baptism. You who have read the Bible must know that that is Bible doctrine. What does it matter if it is not in the same words that I use, it is none the less true that it was baptized for the remission of sins. The Lord said, 'I will deluge (or immerse) the earth in water for the remission of the sins of the people'; or if you will allow me to express myself in a familiar style, to kill all the vermin that were nitting, and breeding, and polluting its body; it was cleansed of its filthiness; and soaked in the water, as long as some of our people ought to soak. The Lord baptized the earth for the remission of sins, and it has been once cleansed for the filthiness that has gone out of it, which was in the inhabitants who dwelt upon its face." (*Journal of Discourses* 1:274.)

"'Brethren and sisters, I wish you to continue in your ways of welldoing; I desire that your minds may be opened more and more to see and understand things as they are. This earth, in its present condition and situation, is not a fit habitation for the sanctified; but it abides the law of its creation, has been baptized with water, will be baptized by fire and the Holy Ghost, and by-and-by will be prepared for the faithful to dwell upon." (JD 8:83.)

Elder Orson Pratt: "Another great change happened nearly two thousand years after the earth was made. It was baptized by water. A great flow of water came, the great deep was broken up, the windows of heaven were opened from on high, and the waters prevailed upon the face of the earth, sweeping away all wickedness and transgression—a similitude of baptism for the remission of sins. God requires the children of men to be baptized. What for? For the remission of sins. So he required our globe to be baptized by a flow of water, and all of its sins were washed away, not one sin remaining." (JD 21:323.)

"Both man and the earth are redeemed from the original sin without ordinances; but soon we find new sins committed by the fallen sons of Adam, and the earth became corrupted before the Lord by their transgressions. It needs redeeming ordinances for these second transgressions. The Lord ordained baptism, or immersion of the earth in water, as a justifying ordinance." (JD 1:291.)

President John Taylor: "The earth, as a part of the creation of God, has fulfilled and will fulfill the measure of its creation. It has been baptized by water, it will be baptized by fire; it will be purified and become celestial, and be a fit place for celestial bodies to inhabit." (*Times and Seasons* 5:408-9.)

President Charles W. Penrose: "Thus the inhabitants of the earth with the few exceptions that are beyond the power of redemption will eventually be saved. And the globe on which they passed their probation, having kept the law of its being, will come into remembrance before its Maker. It will die like its products. But it will be quickened again and resurrected in the celestial glory.

"It has been born of water, it will also be born of the Spirit, purified by fire from all the corruptions that once defiled it, developed into its perfections as one of the family of worlds fitted for the Creator's presence, all its latent light awakened into scintillating action, it will move up into its place among the orbs governed by celestial time, and shining 'like a sea of glass mingled with fire,' every tint and color of the heavenly bow radiating from its surface, the ransomed of the Lord will dwell upon it." (*The Contributor* 2:364.)

Chapter Thirteen

IT WAS
A MIRACLE

Critics of the "flood story" raise many objections. Among them are:

1. The ark was too small to hold all the animal species in the world.

2. Noah could not physically have rounded up creatures from every part of the earth.

3. Noah could not have carried enough food to last during the months when the flood was in progress.

4. The stench from all the animals would have been unbearable.

And so they go on.

We must realize that we do not have the full account of the flood and the ark and its inhabitants. The few hundred words in the Bible on the entire life of Noah are sketchy at most. One thing we must remember is that God was at the helm—and He is a God of miracles!

Other things He has done on earth have seemed to be impossible when judged from the human point of view, and because of this, critics have condemned certain scriptural records, called them myths, and at best put them in the category of legend.

A few cases in point:

The taking of the city of Enoch, with all its people, into heaven is a miracle that few people, especially Bible critics, are willing to accept. Yet it was so. That entire city was taken into heaven. Enoch looked down upon the earth from his high vantage point and could see what was going on—this by the gift and power of God. That city will return to earth again—before the Millennium—as one event in connection with the second coming of Christ. And the people will come with it, and they will meet others here on earth and rejoice with them. (Moses 7:62-64.)

Do we believe it? Is this any less a miracle than the flood? Is it harder to believe? Yet it is all true. The scriptures verify the city of Enoch account over and over.

When the Savior identified himself to the Prophet Joseph Smith, he said: "I am the same which spake, and the world was made, and all things came by me. I am the same which have taken the Zion of Enoch into mine own bosom; and verily, I say, even as many as have believed in my name, for I am Christ, and in mine own name, by the virtue of the blood which I have spilt, have I pleaded before the Father for them." (D&C 38:3-4.)

Incidents such as this and the flood are beyond the understanding of "the spirit of man." This is another case in point to illustrate what the Apostle Paul meant when he said:

"For what man knoweth the things of a man, save the spirit of man which is in him? even so the things of God knoweth no man, but the Spirit of God. Now we have received, not the spirit of the world, but the spirit which is of God; that we might know the things that are freely given to us of God. Which things also we speak, not in the words which man's wisdom teacheth, but which the Holy Ghost teacheth; comparing spiritual things with spiritual.

"But the natural man receiveth not the things of the Spirit of God: for they are foolishness unto him: neither can he know them, because they are spiritually discerned." (1 Corinthians 2:11-14.)

One of the greatest undertakings of all time was the departure of the Twelve Tribes of Israel from Egypt, a multitude of people with all their flocks and herds. We emphasize the flocks and herds in this instance. Everyone must understand, and certainly western range people know full well, how slowly cattle and sheep move along a highway.

Tourists know about this, too. They have been caught on the public roads of western states and had to wait for seemingly interminable periods while the slow-moving animals went by, some of them stopping to graze by the roadside, others going off in different directions and having to be brought back by cowboys or herders' dogs.

In the book of Numbers it is reported that the Israelites had with them 337,000 head of sheep and 36,000 head of cattle. And yet they moved faster than Pharaoh's army! How could it be? Only by a miracle! Did not God go with them by day and by night? How were all these people—and all these animals—able to move so quickly? Who can explain it? God worked it out. It was a miracle.

In the Book of Mormon we read that when the people of Limhi fled by night from their Lamanite captors, they took their flocks and herds with them, as did the people of Moses. But the fast-moving armies of the Lamanites could not catch up to them. Wasn't that a miracle?

When Alma's followers fled from the wicked King Noah, what happened? They took their flocks and herds, but they still out-distanced the speeding soldiers pursuing them. "The Lord did strengthen them," the Book of Mormon says, "that the people of king Noah could not overtake them to destroy them. And they fled eight days' journey into the wilderness." (Mosiah 23:2-3.) How do we explain that? Again it was a miracle.

The flood of Noah's time was strictly God's affair. He arranged it, he turned loose the waters upon the earth, and when the time came, he recalled the waters so that the land was dry in an incredibly short time.

The eighth Article of Faith says that we believe the Bible to be the word of God as far as it is translated correctly. All the translations tell the story of the flood in essentially the same manner. All the translations say that the waters went well over the tops of the highest mountains. All the translations declare without any reservation that the flood was universal and that it covered the whole earth. Shall we not believe the Bible account, especially since it is supported fully by modern revelation to the Prophet Joseph Smith and by the Book of Mormon, which was translated from ancient records by the Prophet, using the Urim and Thummim?

If God moved mountains when Enoch commanded it, and if He held back the waters of the Red Sea to allow the Israelites to cross over, and if by the command of Joshua the Jordan River was stopped in its course, could not the Lord have helped the people of Moses, Limhi, and Alma to travel faster than a pursuing army? After all, He created the entire earth!

Didn't Elijah and Elisha stay the waters of the Jordan River in their time? Did they do it by their own power? Didn't Joshua "stop the sun" to lengthen out the day while he finished the battle? Did he do it by his own power? Could any mortal man have done such a thing?

Could the plagues Moses called down upon Pharaoh in his effort to free the Israelites have been other than miracles?

God's work has included mighty natural processes at various times in the history of the world. Noah's deluge was one of them. The flood had a far greater purpose than merely to wipe out Noah's neighbors. God baptized the earth! He would not baptize a portion of it any more than we would be satisfied with a partial immersion if we were baptizing some person. He baptized Adam by a miracle, when there was no one there to perform the ordinance. And now He baptized the earth by His own almighty power, for His own purposes, and the destruction of the wicked was only incidental thereto. And He will yet baptize it with fire, according to the baptismal pattern for us all. (Matthew 3:11; 3 Nephi 19:13.)

Why baptize the earth?

The earth is a living thing. Is there not great sig-
nificance in the scriptural references to the earth? While
Enoch and the Lord discussed the wickedness of men, "it
came to pass that Enoch looked upon the earth; and he
heard a voice from the bowels thereof, saying: Wo, wo is
me, the mother of men; I am pained, I am weary, because
of the wickedness of my children. When shall I rest, and
be cleansed from the filthiness which is gone forth out of
me? When will my Creator sanctify me, that I may rest,
and righteousness for a season abide upon my face?

"And when Enoch heard the earth mourn, he wept,
and cried unto the Lord, saying: O Lord, wilt thou not
have compassion upon the earth? Wilt thou not bless the
children of Noah?

"And it came to pass that Enoch continued his cry
unto the Lord, saying: I ask thee, O Lord, in the name of
thine Only Begotten, even Jesus Christ, that thou wilt
have mercy upon Noah and his seed, that the earth might
never more be covered by the floods." (Moses 7:48-50.)

Note these words coming out of the bowels of the
earth: "When will my Creator sanctify me that I may rest
and righteousness for a season abide upon my face?" Is
that allegory? Would God deal in allegory in circumstances like these? Was not the voice real?

How are men cleansed of their sins? By baptism, and
not only by water, but also by fire and the Holy Ghost.
John the Baptist explained: "I indeed baptize you with
water unto repentance: but he that cometh after me is
mightier than I, whose shoes I am not worthy to bear: he
shall baptize you with the Holy Ghost, and with fire."
(Matthew 3:11.)

The Savior spoke of this to the Nephites when He
said:

"I am the light and the life of the world. I am Alpha
and Omega, the beginning and the end. And ye shall offer

up unto me no more the shedding of blood; yea, your sacrifices and your burnt offerings shall be done away, for I will accept none of your sacrifices and your burnt offerings.

"And ye shall offer for a sacrifice unto me a broken heart and a contrite spirit. And whoso cometh unto me with a broken heart and a contrite spirit, him will I baptize with fire and with the Holy Ghost, even as the Lamanites, because of their faith in me at the time of their conversion, were baptized with fire and with the Holy Ghost, and they knew it not.

"Behold, I have come unto the world to bring redemption unto the world, to save the world from sin. Therefore, whoso repenteth and cometh unto me as a little child, him will I receive, for of such is the kingdom of God. Behold, for such I have laid down my life, and taken it up again; therefore repent, and come unto me ye ends of the earth, and be saved." (3 Nephi 9:18-22.)

Should not the earth—a living thing—be similarly sanctified? It was baptized with water in the flood. Eventually it will be baptized with fire, thus becoming cleansed and sanctified, to be made into a celestial sphere as the eternal home for the righteous. The Lord has told us: "The place where God resides is a great Urim and Thummim. This earth, in its sanctified and immortal state, will be made like unto crystal and will be a Urim and Thummim to the inhabitants who dwell thereon, whereby all things pertaining to an inferior kingdom, or all kingdoms of a lower order, will be manifest to those who dwell on it; and this earth will be Christ's." (D&C 130:8-9.)

When the Lord gave the revelation found in section 88 of the Doctrine and Convenants, He made this further explanation: "And again, verily I say unto you, the earth abideth the law of a celestial kingdom, for it filleth the measure of its creation, and transgresseth not the law—wherefore, it shall be sanctified; yea, notwithstanding it shall die, it shall be quickened again, and shall abide the power by which it is quickened, and the righteous shall inherit it.'' (D&C 88:25-26.)

Let us recognize the miracles of God. Let us see Him walk in his glory as He performs them.

Think of the natural upheavals that will precede and accompany the second coming of Christ. They will be God's miracles: Mountains will topple. Valleys will be raised. Seas will heave beyond their bounds. Earthquakes will cause the earth to reel as a drunkard. An overflowing scourge will come. Tempests will rage. The city of Enoch will return. And for the coming of the Ten Tribes from the land of the north, a highway will be cast up out of the sea.

Miracles? Doesn't God exercise His infinite strength to bring about His own purposes at His own time? With all His divine power, sufficient even to form the galaxies out in space, was He not able to eliminate the animal odors in the ark? If He could feed three million Israelites on manna and quail for forty years, would He not be able to provide food in the ark for 150 days? Who knows how many species of life there were in Noah's day? Who knows whether those now living existed then? Who knows if animal life was actually scattered over the whole earth then? Obviously human life was pretty much confined to a limited area. Was animal life also? It was after the flood that the scriptures say life was scattered over the whole earth. Who knows?

Who knows many things? Why not admit that we do not possess all knowledge, not even a detailed account of the deluge, and give God credit for having the intelligence to accomplish what He had in mind?

Since He had the power to create the earth in the first place, with all its oceans, underground lakes, fountains, and wells, in addition to the rain clouds in the skies, was He not able to control the elements and cause a flood if He wanted to? Is anything too hard for the Lord?

The flood was a miracle. The episode of the animals and other life taken aboard the ark was another miracle. The rise of the waters out of the depths of the earth and the downpour from the skies were God's doing. And so was the subsequent receding of the waters. The deluge covered the earth and the waters receded just as God planned it all. And it was truly a miracle.

Chapter Fourteen

THE SPIRITS IN PRISON

As we have indicated, the entire doctrine of salvation for the dead affirms the fact of the flood of Noah's day.

The people who drowned were taken to a spirit prison, where the Savior visited them between his death and resurrection and taught the gospel to them. This is beautifully and forcefully affirmed by the vision of President Joseph F. Smith, who described it as follows:

"While I was thus engaged, my mind reverted to the writings of the apostle Peter, to the primitive saints scattered abroad throughout Pontus, Galatia, Cappadocia, and other parts of Asia, where the gospel had been preached after the crucifixion of the Lord. I opened the Bible and read the third and fourth chapters of the first epistle of Peter, and as I read I was greatly impressed, more than I had ever been before, with the following passages:

"'For Christ also hath once suffered for sins, the just for the unjust, that he might bring us to God, being put to death in the flesh, but quickened by the Spirit: by which also he went and preached unto the spirits in prison; which sometime were disobedient, when once the long-suffering of God waited in the days of Noah, while the ark was a preparing, wherein few, that is, eight souls were saved by water.' (1 Peter 3:18-20.)

"'For, for this cause was the gospel preached also to them that are dead, that they might be judged according to men in the flesh, but live according to God in the spirit.' (1 Peter 4:6.)

"As I pondered over these things which are written,

the eyes of my understanding were opened, and the Spirit of the Lord rested upon me, and I saw the hosts of the dead, both small and great. And there were gathered together in one place an innumerable company of the spirits of the just, who had been faithful in the testimony of Jesus while they lived in mortality, and who had offered sacrifice in the similitude of the great sacrifice of the Son of God, and had suffered tribulation in their Redeemer's name. All these had departed the mortal life, firm in the hope of a glorious resurrection, through the grace of God the Father and his Only Begotten Son, Jesus Christ.

"I beheld that they were filled with joy and gladness, and were rejoicing together because the day of their deliverance was at hand. They were assembled awaiting the advent of the Son of God into the spirit world, to declare their redemption from the bands of death. Their sleeping dust was to be restored unto its perfect frame, bone to his bone, and the sinews and the flesh upon them, the spirit and the body to be united never again to be divided, that they might receive a fulness of joy.

"While this vast multitude waited and conversed, rejoicing in the hour of their deliverance from the chains of death, the Son of God appeared, declaring liberty to the captives who had been faithful; and there he preached to them the everlasting gospel, the doctrine of the resurrection and the redemption of mankind from the fall, and from individual sins on conditions of repentance." (D&C 138:5-19.)

Reference is also made to these same spirits in the seventy-sixth section of the Doctrine and Covenants, where we read:

"And again, we saw the terrestrial world, and behold and lo, these are they who are of the terrestrial, whose glory differs from that of the church of the Firstborn who have received the fulness of the Father, even as that of the moon differs from the sun in the firmament.

"Behold, these are they who died without law; and also they who are the spirits of men kept in prison, whom the Son visited, and preached the gospel unto them, that they might be judged according to men in the flesh; who received not the testimony of Jesus in the flesh, but afterwards received it." (Verses 71-74.)

Here again is evidence that the Savior did visit these spirits in prison, which in turn affirms the fact of the flood.

Additional proof is seen in this portrayal of events related to the Lord's second coming: "And after this another angel shall sound, which is the second trump; and then cometh the redemption of those who are Christ's at his coming; who have received their part in that prison which is prepared for them, that they might receive the gospel, and be judged according to men in the flesh." (D&C 88:99.)

Further reference to the spirits in prison is made by the Prophet Joseph Smith, who wrote about the work for the dead: "Brethren, shall we not go on in so great a cause? Go forward and not backward. Courage, brethren; and on, on to the victory! Let your hearts rejoice, and be exceedingly glad. Let the earth break forth into singing. Let the dead speak forth anthems of eternal praise to the King Immanuel, who hath ordained, before the world was, that which would enable us to redeem them out of their prison; for the prisoners shall go free." (D&C 128:22.)

The Nephites were taught about the flood and the reality of Noah and his ministry. When Alma and Amulek warned them of destruction if they failed to repent, they were told: "Yea, and I say unto you that if it were not for the prayers of the righteous, who are now in the land, that ye would even now be visited with utter destruction; yet it would not be by flood, as were the people in the days of Noah, but it would be by famine, and by pestilence, and the sword." (Alma 10:22.)

Chapter Fifteen

WHEN IT WAS OVER

When the flood was over and the ground was dry, Noah and his sons offered sacrifices to the Lord. The Joseph Smith Translation of the Bible says: "And Noah builded an altar unto the Lord, and took of every clean beast, and of every clean fowl, and offered burnt offerings on the altar; and gave thanks unto the Lord, and rejoiced in his heart." (Genesis 9:14.)

One may wonder about Noah offering beasts in sacrifice to the Lord immediately after his emergence from the ark. It will be remembered that although he took two by two of all *unclean* animals, he took seven and seven of the clean ones; thus he had sufficient to allow him to make the sacrifices and yet not interfere with the procreation needed to replenish the earth.

The Lord was pleased with the sacrifice. Noah said, "I will call on the name of the Lord, that he will not again curse the ground any more for man's sake, for the imagination of man's heart is evil from his youth; and that he will not again smite any more every thing living, as he hath done, while the earth remaineth; and, that seed-time and harvest, and cold and heat, and summer and winter, and day and night, may not cease with man.

"And God blessed Noah and his sons, and said unto them, Be fruitful and multiply, and replenish the earth. And the fear of you, and the dread of you shall be upon every beast of the earth, and upon every fowl of the air, upon all that moveth upon the earth, and upon all the fishes of the sea; into your hands are they delivered." (JST, Genesis 9:6-8.)

The Lord answered Noah's prayers. He made a covenant with him that there would be no more floods, and there would always be seed time and harvest. Then He gave him the rainbow in the sky as the sign of the covenant.

"And God spake unto Noah, and to his sons with him, saying, And I, behold, I will establish my covenant with you, which I made upon your father Enoch, concerning your seed after you.

"And it shall come to pass, that every living creature that is with you, of the fowl, and of the cattle, and of the beast of the earth that is with you, which shall go out of the ark, shall not altogether perish; neither shall all flesh be cut off any more by the waters of the flood; neither shall there any more be a flood to destroy the earth. And I will establish my covenant with you, which I made unto Enoch, concerning the remnants of your posterity.

"And God made a covenant with Noah, and said, This shall be the token of the covenant I make between me and you, and for every living creature with you, for perpetual generations; I will set my bow in the cloud; and it shall be for a token of a covenant between me and the earth.

"And it shall come to pass, when I bring a cloud over the earth, that the bow shall be seen in the cloud; and I will remember my covenant, which I have made between me and you, for every living creature of all flesh. And the waters shall no more become a flood to destroy all flesh.

"And the bow shall be in the cloud; and I will look upon it, that I may remember the everlasting covenant, which I made unto thy father Enoch; that, when men should keep all my commandments, Zion should again come on the earth, the city of Enoch which I have caught up unto myself.

"And this is mine everlasting covenant, that when thy posterity shall embrace the truth, and look upward, then shall Zion look downward, and all the heavens shall shake with gladness, and the earth shall tremble with joy; and the general assembly of the church of the firstborn shall come down out of heaven, and possess the earth, and shall have place until the end come. And this is mine everlasting covenant, which I made with thy father Enoch. And the bow shall be in the cloud, and I will establish my covenant unto thee, which I have made between me and thee, for every living creature of all flesh that shall be upon the earth.

"And God said unto Noah, This is the token of the covenant which I have established between me and thee; for all flesh that shall be upon the earth." (JST, Genesis 9:15-25.)

It was a marvelous covenant, and a revelation of what is to happen in the latter days as well, even as was shown to Enoch when he and his city were taken into heaven.

Chapter Sixteen

THE SIN OF MURDER

The Lord gave many commandments to Noah and his sons, and one of the most important taught them how precious is human life. The Lord forbade the unnecessary destruction of any kind of life, although He gave animals, fish, and birds to Noah for food, in addition to grains, fruits, and vegetables. But He especially declared against the loss of human life. Murder must be punished with death! This was the divine decree.

The law came about as the Lord gave instruction regarding the use of meat for food. Said He; "Every moving thing that liveth shall be meat for you; even as the green herb have I given you all things. But, the blood of all flesh which I have given you for meat, shall be shed upon the ground, which taketh life thereof, and the blood ye shall not eat. And surely, blood shall not be shed, only for meat, to save your lives; and the blood of every beast will I require at thy hands." (JST, Genesis 9:9-11.)

Other Bible translations are as much to the point. Says the Revised Standard Version: "Every moving thing that lives shall be food for you; and as I gave you the green plants, I give you everything." But the Lord made this prohibition: "Only you shall not eat the flesh with its life, that is, its blood." (Genesis 9:3-4.)

The New World Translation says: "Into your hand they are now given. Every moving animal that is alive may serve as food for you. As in the case of green vegetation, I do give it all to you. Only flesh with its soul—its blood—you must not eat." (Genesis 9:2-4.)

The Knox Translation: "This creation that lives and

moves is to provide food for you; I make it all over to you, by the same title as the herbs that have growth. Only, you must not eat the flesh with the blood still in it." (Genesis 9:3-4.)

Then the Lord spoke of murder: Neither man nor beast may kill a human being; otherwise he—even the beast—will be held accountable.

Said the Lord in Joseph Smith's inspired version: "Whoso sheddeth man's blood, by man shall his blood be shed; for man shall not shed the blood of man. For a commandment I give, that every man's brother shall preserve the life of man, for in mine own image have I made man." (Genesis 9:12-13.)

The Revised Standard Version reads: "For your lifeblood I will surely require a reckoning; of every beast I will require it and of man; of every man's brother I will require the life of man. Whoever sheds the blood of man, by man shall his blood be shed; for God made man in his own image." (Genesis 9:5-6.)

The Knox Version says: "The shedder of your own life blood shall be held to account for it, whether man or beast. Whoever takes the life of his brother-man shall answer for it to me. Man was made in God's image and whoever sheds man's blood must shed his own in return."

And this comes from the New World Translation: "Only flesh with its soul—its blood—you must not eat. And besides that, your blood of your souls shall I ask back. From the hand of every living creature shall I ask it back; and from the hand of man, from the hand of each one who is his brother, shall I ask back the soul of man. Anyone shedding man's blood, by man will his own blood be shed, for in God's image he made man." (Genesis 9:4-7.)

In the scriptures according to the Masoretic text we read: "Every moving thing that liveth shall be for food for you; as the green herb have I given you all. Only flesh with the life thereof, which is the blood thereof, shall ye not eat. And surely your blood of your lives will I require; at the hand of every beast will I require it; and at the hand of man, even at the hand of every man's brother will I require the life of man. Whoso sheddeth man's blood, by man shall his blood be shed; for in the image of God made He man.'' (Genesis 9:3-7.)

So in this instruction we have the following:

1. There shall be no murder.

2. Capital punishment was decreed for this crime.

3. Whatever person or whatever animal takes a human life will be held accountable by the Almighty.

4. Animal meat is allowed for the use of man.

5. The blood of animals must not be used as food, and no flesh with the blood still within it may be eaten.

What great value the Lord puts upon human life! And why? Because man is made in the image of God. So sacred is that image—so vital is our relationship to God—so precious is life!

Chapter Seventeen

NOAH'S DESCENDANTS

Noah and his sons had children after the flood, and they in turn multiplied in the earth and became numerous. It is interesting to note the names of some of them. Among the descendants of Japheth are Gomer, Magog, Tubal, Meshech, Togarmah, and Tarshish. These names are particularly interesting because they appear in the predictions of Ezekiel with regard to the battle of Armegeddon, which will be fought before the coming of the Lord. They are carried down to the present day.

When Ezekiel talks about the battle leading up to Christ's appearance in Palestine at the "end of the world," he says:

"And the word of the Lord came unto me, saying, Son of man, set thy face against Gog, the land of Magog, the chief prince of Meshech and Tubal, and prophesy against him, and say, Thus saith the Lord God; Behold, I am against thee, O Gog, the chief prince of Meshech and Tubal:

"And I will turn thee back, and put hooks into thy jaws, and I will bring thee forth, and all thine army, horses and horsemen, all of them clothed with all sorts of armour, even a great company with bucklers and shields, all of them handling swords: Persia, Ethiopia, and Libya with them; all of them with shield and helmet: Gomer, and all his bands; the house of Togarmah of the north quarters, and all his bands; and many people with thee.

"Be thou prepared, and prepare for thyself, thou, and all thy company that are assembled unto thee, and be thou a guard unto thee." (Ezekiel 38:1-7.)

These are people who anciently lived in the areas of the Black and Caspian seas and the Caucasus region, and many still live there today.

The Lord declared his opposition to these people in their invasion of Palestine; we read:

"Therefore, thou son of man, prophesy against Gog, and say, Thus saith the Lord God; Behold, I am against thee, O Gog, the chief prince of Meshech and Tubal: And I will turn thee back, and leave but the sixth part of thee, and will cause thee to come up from the north parts, and will bring thee upon the mountains of Israel: and I will smite thy bow out of thy left hand, and will cause thine arrows to fall out of thy right hand.

"Thou shalt fall upon the mountains of Israel, thou, and all thy bands, and the people that is with thee: I will give thee unto the ravenous birds of every sort, and to the beasts of the field to be devoured. Thou shalt fall upon the open field: for I have spoken it, saith the Lord God. And I will send a fire on Magog, and among them that dwell carelessly in the isles: and they shall know that I am the Lord.

"So will I make my holy name known in the midst of my people Israel; and I will not let them pollute my holy name any more: and the heathen shall know that I am the Lord, the Holy One in Israel." (Ezekiel 39:1-7.)

Canaan, of course, comes through Ham, and Noah's curse rests upon him:

"And Noah began to be an husbandman, and he planted a vineyard: and he drank of the wine, and was drunken; and he was uncovered within his tent.

"And Ham, the father of Canaan, saw the nakedness of his father, and told his two brethren without. And Shem and Japheth took a garment, and laid it upon both their shoulders, and went backward, and covered the nakedness of their father; and their faces were backward, and they saw not their father's nakedness.

"And Noah awoke from his wine, and knew what his younger son had done unto him. And he said, Cursed be Canaan; a servant of servants shall he be unto his brethren. And he said, Blessed be the Lord God of Shem; and Canaan shall be his servant. God shall enlarge Japheth, and he shall dwell in the tents of Shem; and Canaan shall be his servant." (Genesis 9:20-27.)

Another descendant of Noah was Nimrod, a grandson of Ham and son of Cush. We read that Nimrod "began to be a mighty one in the earth. He was a mighty hunter before the Lord: wherefore it is said, Even as Nimrod the mighty hunter before the Lord. And the beginning of his kingdom was Babel, and Erech, and Accad, and Calneh, in the land of Shinar. Out of that land went forth Asshur, and builded Nineveh." (Genesis 10:8-12.)

It was at Babel, of course, that the languages were confused.

This note gives some idea of the antiquity of Nineveh, which was recently excavated by archeologists; they found rich treasures there, including whole libraries of cuneiform records, one of the most valuable finds in the Middle East.

Eber, the ancestor of the Hebrews, was a descendant of Noah's son Shem, and of Eber was born Peleg, in whose days "the earth was divided." (Genesis 10:25.)

The phrase "the earth was divided" is also found in 1 Chronicles 1:19. President Joseph Fielding Smith explains:

"Joseph Smith gave this inspired summary of latter-day events: 'There shall be famine, and pestilence, and earthquake in divers places; and the prophets have declared that the valleys should rise; that the mountains should be laid low; that a great earthquake should be, the sun should become black as sack-cloth of hair, and the moon turned into blood; yea, the Eternal God hath declared that the great deep shall roll back into the north

countries and that the land of Zion and the land of
Jerusalem shall be joined together, as they were before
they were divided in the days of Peleg. No wonder the
mind starts at the sound of the last days!'

"Here the Prophet tells us that the dividing of the
earth was in the days of Peleg. When Christ comes, it will
be brought back again as it was before it was divided."
(*Doctrines of Salvation* 1:84-85.)

President Smith also wrote:

"The Bible teaches us that in the beginning all the
water was in one place. Therefore all the land must have
been in one place. (Genesis 1:9.) There was not an Eastern and a Western Hemisphere at the time of Adam. . . .

"In the beginning the land surface was one vast continent; there came a time when it was divided, and other
continents were formed and the Western Hemisphere
came into existence, but that was long after the time of
Adam. . . .

"If one should take a map showing the Western and
the Eastern hemispheres, and study them, one would
clearly see how today they might be fitted together. Well,
that day will come, for, as the earth was divided, so shall
it in the restoration be brought back to its original form
again, with all the land surface in one place." (*Answers to
Gospel Questions* 4:21-23.)

President Smith also refers to other changes mentioned in the following scriptures.

From Ezekiel: "For in my jealousy and in the fire of
my wrath have I spoken, Surely in that day there shall be
a great shaking in the land of Israel; so that the fishes of
the sea, and the fowls of the heaven, and the beasts of the
field, and all creeping things that creep upon the earth,
and all the men that are upon the face of the earth, shall
shake at my presence, and the mountains shall be thrown
down, and the steep places shall fall, and every wall shall
fall to the ground." (Ezekiel 38:19-20.)

From John the Revelator: "And every island fled away, and the mountains were not found." (Revelations 16:20.)

From the Doctrine and Covenants: "And he shall utter his voice out of Zion, and he shall speak from Jerusalem, and his voice shall be heard among all people; and it shall be a voice as the voice of many waters, and as the voice of a great thunder, which shall break down the mountains, and the valleys should not be found.

"He shall command the great deep, and it shall be driven back into the north countries, and the islands shall become one land; and the land of Jerusalem and the land of Zion shall be turned back into their own place, and the earth shall be like as it was in the days before it was divided." (D&C 133:21-24.)

Chapter Eighteen

THE JAREDITE BARGES

In a manner, the Jaredite barges were likened to Noah's ark. Although the barges were smaller and were suitable for underwater travel, there were some similarities of which the scriptures speak.

Where did the Jaredites come from, and what was their relationship to Noah and his descendants after the flood?

It will be remembered that "God blessed Noah and his sons, and said unto them, Be fruitful, and multiply, and replenish the earth. And the fear of you and the dread of you shall be upon every beast of the earth, and upon every fowl of the air, upon all that moveth upon the earth, and upon all the fishes of the sea; into your hand are they delivered." (Genesis 9:1-2.)

After giving the descent of the offspring of Noah, the scripture continues: "These are the families of the sons of Noah, after their generations, in their nations: and by these were the nations divided in the earth after the flood." (Genesis 10:32.)

The record then says: "And the whole earth was of one language, and of one speech.

"And it came to pass, as they journeyed from the east, that they found a plain in the land of Shinar; and they dwelt there. And they said one to another, Go to, let us make brick, and burn them throughly. And they had brick for stone, and slime had they for morter. And they said, Go to, let us build us a city and a tower, whose top may reach unto heaven; and let us make us a name, lest we be scattered abroad upon the face of the whole earth.

"And the Lord came down to see the city and the tower, which the children of men builded. And the Lord said, Behold, the people is one, and they have all one language; and this they begin to do: and now nothing will be restrained from them, which they have imagined to do. Go to, let us go down, and there confound their language, that they may not understand one another's speech.

"So the Lord scattered them abroad from thence upon the face of all the earth: and they left off to build the city. Therefore is the name of it called Babel; because the Lord did there confound the language of all the earth: and from thence did the Lord scatter them abroad upon the face of all the earth." (Genesis 11:1-9.)

Here begins the story of Jared and his family, which is recorded in the Book of Mormon:

"And Kib was the son of Orihah, who was the son of Jared; which Jared came forth with his brother and their families, with some others and their families, from the great tower, at the time the Lord confounded the language of the people, and swore in his wrath that they should be scattered upon all the face of the earth; and according to the word of the Lord the people were scattered.

"And the brother of Jared being a large and mighty man, and a man highly favored of the Lord, Jared, his brother, said unto him: Cry unto the Lord, that he will not confound us that we may not understand our words.

"And it came to pass that the brother of Jared did cry unto the Lord, and the Lord had compassion upon Jared; therefore he did not confound the language of Jared; and Jared and his brother were not confounded.

"Then Jared said unto his brother: Cry again unto the Lord, and it may be that he will turn away his anger from them who are our friends, that he confound not their language.

"And it came to pass that the brother of Jared did cry unto the Lord, and the Lord had compassion upon their friends and their families also, that they were not confounded." (Ether 1:32-37.)

The brother of Jared then asked the Lord to reveal where He would like the family to go. The Lord replied: "Go to and gather together thy flocks, both male and female, of every kind; and also of the seed of the earth of every kind; and thy families; and also Jared thy brother and his family; and also thy friends and their families, and the friends of Jared and their families.

"And when thou hast done this thou shalt go at the head of them down into the valley which is northward. And there will I meet thee, and I will go before thee into a land which is choice above all the lands of the earth. And there will I bless thee and thy seed, and raise up unto me of thy seed, and of the seed of thy brother, and they who shall go with thee, a great nation. And there shall be none greater than the nation which I will raise up unto me of thy seed, upon all the face of the earth. And thus I will do unto thee because this long time ye have cried unto me." (Ether 1:41-43.)

The journey required the building of ships or barges.

"And the Lord said: Go to work and build, after the manner of barges which ye have hitherto built. And it came to pass that the brother of Jared did go to work, and also his brethren, and built barges after the manner which they had built, according to the instructions of the Lord. And they were small, and they were light upon the water, even like unto the lightness of a fowl upon the water.

"And they were built after a manner that they were exceeding tight, even that they would hold water like unto a dish; and the bottom thereof was tight like unto a dish; and the sides thereof were tight like unto a dish; and the ends thereof were peaked; and the top thereof was tight like unto a dish; and the length thereof was the length of a tree; and the door thereof, when it was shut, was tight like unto a dish." (Ether 2:16-17.)

The record now says: "And it came to pass that when they had prepared all manner of food, that thereby they might subsist upon the water, and also food for their flocks and herds, and whatsoever beast or animal or fowl that they should carry with them—and it came to pass that when they had done all these things they got aboard of their vessels or barges, and set forth into the sea, commending themselves unto the Lord their God." (Ether 6:4.)

The barges were as sturdy and water-tight as Noah's ark. "And it came to pass that when they were buried in the deep there was no water that could hurt them, their vessels being tight like unto a dish, and also they were tight like unto the ark of Noah; therefore when they were encompassed about by many waters they did cry unto the Lord, and he did bring them forth again upon the top of the waters." (Ether 6:7.)

Here was another overseas journey that included transportation of animals and people, a journey that took a year in which only a miracle could have kept the people and their cargo alive.

Think of the care of those animals for a year, of their food, ventilation inside the craft, and the health of both people and beasts. Only a miracle could have done it. And only a miracle did. It was in the same class as the voyage of the ark. It all comes back again to the matter of faith in the scriptures as against the rationale of the critics. Of course, the wisdom of God seems like foolishness to men who ridicule these accounts of miracles in transportation that literally defy all the logic of the scholars.

Acceptance of the exodus of Moses, the escapes of people in the Book of Mormon, the seemingly impossible conditions pertaining to the flood and the ark, and the account of the people of Jared—all this requires faith in the sacred word, remembering that the wisdom of man is foolishness to God and that the Almighty can do all things.

He is not bound by the physical restrictions of human beings. Didn't He create the world in the first place?

It is part of our religion to believe the scriptures, which are plain and clear on these miraculous events. For each individual the question is, simply, which shall we believe—the word of God or the speculations of men?

Chapter Nineteen

TRADITIONS
FROM ELSEWHERE

Traditions of the flood as they exist among both ancient and modern peoples are numerous. Nearly all of them have some grain of truth, although no doubt they have seen much change over the generations.

One authority gives this interesting information:

"The historicity of the Biblical Flood account is confirmed by the tradition existing in all places and at all times as to the occurrence of a similar catastrophe. F. von Schwarz (Sintfluth und Völkerwanderungen, pp. 8-18) enumerates sixty-three such Flood stories which are in his opinion independent of the Biblical account. R. Andree (Die Flutsagen ethnographisch betrachtet) discusses eighty-eight different Flood stories, and considers sixty-two of them as independent of the Chaldee and Hebrew tradition. Moreover, these stories extend through all the races of the earth excepting the African; these are excepted, not because it is certain that they do not possess any Flood traditions, but because their traditions have not as yet been sufficiently investigated.

"Lenormant pronounces the Flood story as the most universal tradition in the history of primitive man, and Franz Delitzsch was of opinion that we might as well consider the history of Alexander the Great a myth, as to call the Flood tradition a fable. It would, indeed, be a greater miracle than that of the Deluge itself, if the various and different conditions surrounding the several nations of the earth had produced among them a tradition substantially identical. Opposite causes would have produced the same effect." (*The Catholic Encyclopedia* 4:704.)

This same authority comments further on the flood:

"There are also certain scientific considerations which oppose the view that the Flood was geographically universal. Not that science opposes any difficulty insuperable to the power of God; but it draws attention to a number of most extraordinary, if not miraculous phenomena involved in the admission of a geographically universal Deluge.

"First, no such geological traces can be found as ought to have been left by a universal Deluge; for the catastrophe connected with the beginning of the ice-age, or the geological deluge, must not be connected with the Biblical.

"Secondly, the amount of water required by a universal Deluge, as described in the Bible, cannot be accounted for by the data furnished in the Biblical account. If the surface of the earth, in round numbers, amounts to 510,000,000 square kilometres, and if the elevation of the highest mountains reaches about 9000 metres, the water required by the Biblical Flood, if it be universal, amounts to about 4,600,000,000 cubic kilometres. Now, a forty days' rain, ten times more copious than the most violent rainfall known to us, will raise the level of the sea only about 800 metres; since the height to be attained is about 9000 metres, there is still a gap to be filled by unknown sources amounting to a height of more than 8000 metres, in order to raise the water to the level of the greatest mountains.

"Thirdly, if the Biblical Deluge was geographically universal, the sea water and the fresh water would mix to such an extent that neither the marine animals nor the fresh-water animals could have lived in the mixture without a miracle.

"Fourthly, there are serious difficulties connected with the animals in the ark, if the Flood was geographically universal: How were they brought to Noe from the remote regions of the earth in which they lived? How could eight persons take care of such an array of beasts? Where did they obtain the food necessary for all the animals? How could the arctic animals live with those of the torrid zone for a whole year and under the same roof?

"No Catholic commentator will repudiate an explanation merely for fear of having to admit a miracle; but no Catholic has a right to admit Biblical miracles which are not well attested either by Scripture or tradition." (Ibid. pp. 704-5.)

The experts go far afield when they refuse to acknowledge the hand of God in great natural events.

President Anthony W. Ivins, counselor to President Heber J. Grant in the First Presidency, was an authority on American Indians. He traveled widely among them, learned some of their languages, was the recipient of their full confidence, and was himself a great missionary among them. His labors and travels were particularly extensive in Mexico and Central America. Out of his vast contact with the natives there he wrote the following for *Liahona, the Elders' Journal* in 1910 concerning traditions of the flood known among those peoples.

"Mexican mythology relates that there was war in Heaven—that Zontemonque rebelled and led away a host of spirits and that because of his rebellion he was cast out with his followers; the Suchiquecal was tempted and disobeyed the command of the Creator by gathering roses from a tree and that because of sin Yztlacoliuhqui became blind and naked, and that misery and disgrace came to all of their descendants.

"The belief that the earth was once deluged with water and all of its inhabitants destroyed except a few who were miraculously preserved is almost universal.

"The Mexicans tell us that the earth was deluged with water, and that Coxcox and his wife Xochiquetzal made a boat from the trunk of a bald cypress in which they were saved. The Tarascos tell us that the earth was deluged with water and that Tezpi and his family were saved by embarking in a vessel which they had made. That when the waters receded a vulture was sent out, but it feasted on the bodies of those who had been drowned, and did not return. A humming-bird was sent out which returned with a green leaf in its beak and Tepzi knew that the dry land had appeared.

"The Pimas tell us that the earth was deluged with water and the Papogos say that Moctazuma was the only person to escape a great flood. The Californians relate that Taylor Peak is the point upon which their fathers took refuge and were saved when all other people were destroyed with water. The Thlinkeets say that many people were saved from a great deluge by taking refuge in a floating building, and that when the waters receded it struck upon a rock and was broken in twain. The Peruvians relate that for five days the sun was obscured during which time the windows of heaven were opened and the earth deluged; that a shepherd and his family with many animals took refuge on Mount Ancasmarca. As the water rose the mountain rose with it and floated. When the waters subsided the shepherd went forth and again peopled the earth.

"Among many of the Indians the rainbow is regarded as a sign that the earth will never again be submerged. The Peruvians say that the ends of the rainbow rest upon the waters of the sea and hold them down to their proper level.

"Connected with these flood myths is the general belief that after the waters subsided the people undertook the construction of a great tower which should be so high that the waters could never reach the top.

"The Mexicans say that after the deluge the people began to build an artificial mountain, but the anger of the gods was incurred and they slew many of the builders and the work stopped. The Californians tell us that after the deluge the people undertook the construction of a great tower in order that they might have a place of refuge in case the earth were again submerged.

"Such are some of the wonderful traditions preserved among the Indians, pointing to a Hebrew origin." (*Liahona* 8 [July 12, 1910]: 51-52.)

Chapter Twenty

THE CHOICE BEFORE US

God gave man his free agency and made him lord over the whole earth. He gave him an inquiring mind with a great curiosity about life and physical conditions here on earth.

So man became an explorer, a researcher. He became determined to find out "what makes things tick." He wanted to know about origins and purposes. What is life? Where did we come from? Were we always human? Is there life after death? Is there really a divine Being, a Creator?

This driving urge for learning took him far beyond the earth. Space beckoned him. Men went to the moon and came back to tell the tale. Missiles were sent out to Saturn and beyond. Photographs of distant planets and galaxies were obtained as by a miracle.

His studies entered many fields. That is why we have so many inventions for our convenience today. We have new uses for electricity; we have computers, jet airplanes, and fast trains. We have robots to do heavy or tedious work. We travel beneath the surface of the sea in various kinds of underwater conveyances, including submarines for war and other vehicles to study the ocean floor. There seems to be no end to the curiosity and achievements of man. Archaeology and anthropology have produced fascinating facts and theories. Astronomy has opened our eyes to objects in space trillions of light years away. And all of this comes through the blessing of heaven.

The Lord has advised Latter-day Saints to keep up with the times, to improve their education and obtain more knowledge to make them more efficient in their work.

So it was that He urged the Prophet Joseph Smith and the Saints to seek knowledge "out of the best books." His command to acquire knowledge and to "teach one another" is a most interesting one. Leaving no restrictions, He said:

"Teach ye diligently and my grace shall attend you, that you may be instructed more perfectly in theory, in principle, in doctrine, in the law of the gospel, in all things that pertain unto the kingdom of God, that are expedient for you to understand;

"Of things both in heaven and in the earth, and under the earth; things which have been, things which are, things which must shortly come to pass; things which are at home, things which are abroad; the wars and the perplexities of the nations, and the judgments which are on the land; and a knowledge also of countries and of kingdoms." (D&C 88:78-79.)

At another time he gave revelation in which he told his Saints to "study and learn, and become acquainted with all good books, and with languages, tongues, and people." (D&C 90:15.)

It is believed that the great discoveries and inventions of the present day are a result of the Spirit of God inspiring "all flesh," as reported by the prophet Joel. (Joel 2:28.)

Inventions have come as the Church has required them in its rapid growth. When fast travel was needed to service distant regions of the earth, jet planes were made available. When means were needed to handle the rapidly increasing membership records and whole libraries of names for temple and genealogical work, computers came. When there was a need for extensive coverage by the spoken word and by picture, radio and television and satellites came.

The Lord has inspired inventors of the world to produce their work not only for the good of mankind, but also and especially for the onward movement of His kingdom. Where the Church is, these enlightening processes are put to work for the extension of the Lord's kingdom.

Great as men are in their calculations and research, however, and wide as is their exploration with microscopes, telescopes, and the spade of the archaeologist, their deductions are not always correct. One of the admirable attributes of great scientific men is their willingness to discard old hypotheses when new truth is found. It is a mark of progress. There are still deductions and unproven theories that are subject to serious question. Particularly are these ideas questionable when they invade the Lord's domain, such as the Creation, the flood of Noah's day, life after death, and even the resurrection.

Latter-day Saints do seek knowledge. We strongly advocate study, research, and education; but we cannot agree with misguided conclusions that defy the scriptures and seem to refute revelation. Revelation is real! Revelation is sure!

The testimony of The Church of Jesus Christ of Latter-day Saints is that—God does live!

Jesus of Nazareth lives! He is the divine Son of God, and our Redeemer.

Creation came about by divine means as set forth in the holy scriptures.

There was a flood. It was a miracle that worldly men do not as yet understand.

There was an ark, and there was a mighty prophet named Noah.

God has spoken in our day, and through modern revelation we know many things that research cannot discover.

We know that God lives because our modern prophets have seen Him.

We know that Jesus Christ lives because our modern prophets have seen Him also and have communed with Him, face to face, as one man speaks to another.

We know that God created all things because he has revealed this fact to our modern prophet, Joseph Smith, Jr.

For the same reason, we know there was a flood.

And we know by modern revelation that Noah, builder of the ark, was a mighty being in the pre-earth world, second only to Adam, or Michael, and third in the priesthood line from the Lord Jesus Christ. He was Gabriel, who announced the forthcoming birth of the Savior of the world. Did he not then, in fact, introduce the Christian era?

And God—is He not a mighty miracle worker, far exceeding the feeble comprehension of man?

INDEX

Adam, 1-3, 8-9, 15
Alma, followers of, 60-61
America as land of promise,
   12-13, 35-37
American Translation, 28
Animals, 52-53, 59-60, 72-74
Ararat, Mount, 53
Ark: mentioned in Koran, 10;
   path of, 37; seen by Enoch in
   vision, 41; design of, 46;
   boarding of, 47; in different translations, 49; speculations on, 51; preparations
   for, 52-53; during flood, 54;
   remains of, 55; objections to,
   58, 86-87; miracles related to,
   64-65; compared to Jaredite
   barges, 80, 83; in Indian
   mythology, 87-89
Armageddon, 75-76
Armenia, 53-54

Babel, 77, 80-81, 88-89
Baptism, flood as, 55-57, 61-62
Baptism of fire, 62-64
Barges, Jaredite, 82-83
Blood, shedding of, 72-74
Book of Moses, 32, 38-39

Canaan, 76-77
Church of Jesus Christ of
   Latter-day Saints, inventions
   for, 91-92
City of Enoch. *See* Zion
Constitution of United States, 12
Creation, 39, 92-93
Cyrus the Great, 11

Dove, 50-51, 53

Earth: necessity for cleansing of,
   3, 62; baptized by flood,
   55-57, 61; to be baptized by
   fire, 62-64; dividing of, 77-78
Eber, 77
Egypt, 7, 13-14
Elisabeth, 6-8
Enoch: mission of, 16-19, 24;
   and Zion, 19-21, 58-59; lineage
   of, 22-23, 39-42; acceptance
   of, 39-40; visions of, 40-42,
   62; the Lord's covenants with,
   41-42, 70-71
Exodus, 59-61

Flood: one of three crises, 1; to
   cleanse the world by baptism,
   3-4, 36, 55-57, 61-62; conditions for, 23-24; scriptural
   references to, 32-35, 40-43;
   seen by Enoch in vision,
   40-43; Noah warned of, 42-43;
   problems with, 45, 86-87;
   Jerusalem Bible account of,
   45-48, 50-51; account of, in
   different translations, 49-51;
   speculations on, 51; abating
   of, 53-54; as miracle, 64-65,
   92-93; affirmed by Savior's
   visit to spirit world, 66-68;
   affirmed by traditions, 85;
   in Indian mythology, 87-89;
   testimony of, 92-93
Forewarnings of flood, 32, 34-35

Gabriel: chosen to become
   Noah, 2-4, 15; opened
   Christian era, 5-8; appeared
   to Joseph Smith, 8-9; Arab
   view of, 9; Noah as, 93

with, 53, 70-71; during and
after flood, 53-54; objections
to, 58; built an altar, 69;
commandment to, on murder,
72-74; descendants of, 75-77,
80; Indian names for and
stories of, 87-89; testimony of,
92-93
Noah, King, 60

Peleg, 77-78
Penrose, Charles W., 56-57
Pratt, Orson, 56
Premortality, 2-4, 14-15
Prison house, 40-41. *See also*
Spirit world

Rainbow, 70-71, 88-89
Raven, 50, 53
Revised Standard Version, 49,
72-73
Roman Catholic Knox Transla-
tion, 28, 49, 72-73

Scriptures affirm Noah and
flood, 38
Shem, 23, 25-26, 51, 76-77
Smith, Joseph: identified Adam
and Noah, 2; Gabriel appeared
to, 8-9; on preordination, 14;
received revelation affirming
Noah and flood, 38, 43-44;
refers to spirit prison, 68
Smith, Joseph F., vision of,

of spirit prison, 66-67
Smith, Joseph Fielding: on
premortality, 14-15; on people
at time of Noah, 19-20; on
three great cities, 20-21; on
flood as baptism, 55; on last
days and dividing of earth,
77-79
Son of God visits spirit world,
67-68
Sons of God: Noah and sons
as, 25-27, 29-30; misunderstanding about, 27-29; who
are, 30-31
Spirit of God, 16-17, 59
Spirit world, 66-68. *See also*
Prison house

Taylor, John, 56
Togarmah, 75
Traditions with flood account,
85, 87-89
Translations, differing, of Bible,
27-29, 49-51, 60-61
Tubal, 75-76

Wickedness of antediluvian
people, 20, 25

Young, Brigham, 55-56

Zacharias, 7-8
Zion, 19-21, 58-59, 78-79. *See
also* New Jerusalem